AQA STUDY G

GCSE 9–1
ROMEO & JULIET

BY WILLIAM SHAKESPEARE

SCHOLASTIC

Author Richard Durant

Series Consultants Richard Durant and Cindy Torn

Reviewer Rob Pollard

Editorial team Rachel Morgan, Audrey Stokes, Camilla Erskine, Lesley Densham, Mary Colson, Louise Titley

Typesetting Oxford Designers and Illustrators

Cover design Nicolle Thomas and Neil Salt

App development Hannah Barnett, Phil Crothers and RAIOSOFT International Pvt Ltd

Acknowledgements

Illustration Niall Harding/Oxford Designers & Illustrators

Photographs page 12: mask, Ann Baldwin/Shutterstock; crown, zimmytws/Shutterstock; page 15: antique book, Neil Lang/Shutterstock; page 16: carnival mask, HannaMonika/Shutterstock; page 16 and 68: stars, Zacarias Pereira da Mata/Shutterstock; page 17: angel's wings, TracieGrant/Shutterstock; page 20: cupid, Natwood/Shutterstock; pages 21 and 74: rose, Hong Vo/Shutterstock; page 25: Juliet's balcony, Nikolay Antonov/Shutterstock; page 26: medicinal herbs, Alexander Raths/Shutterstock; page 30: gold rings, dencg/Shutterstock; page 38: teardrop, LedyX/Shutterstock; page 46: glass bottle, Merkushev Vasiliy/Shutterstock; page 48: brown bottle, Levent ALBAS/Shutterstock; pages 50 and 66: cross, Lunatictm/Shutterstock; page 51: man in cloak, andreiuc88/Shutterstock; page 52: green bottle, Alistair Scott/Shutterstock; page 58: dagger, Luuuusa/Shutterstock; pages 67 and 75: earring, Kiselev Andrey Valerevich/Shutterstock; page 70: letters, PGMart/Shutterstock; page 72: gravestone, Jason Salmon/Shutterstock; page 77: swords, gdvcom/Shutterstock; page 78: tragedy mask, A.B.G./Shutterstock; pages 80 and 81: masks, Alfmaler/Shutterstock; page 83: girl doing exam, Monkey Business Images/Shutterstock; page 87: notepad and pen, TRINACRIA PHOTO/Shutterstock

Designed using Adobe InDesign

Published by Scholastic Education, an imprint of Scholastic Ltd, Book End, Range Road, Witney, Oxfordshire, OX29 0YD
Registered office: Westfield Road, Southam, Warwickshire CV47 0RA
www.scholastic.co.uk

Printed by Bell and Bain
© 2019 Scholastic Ltd
3 4 5 6 7 8 9   9 0 1 2 3 4 5 6 7 8

British Library Cataloguing-in-Publication Data
A catalogue record for this book is available from the British Library.

ISBN 978-1407-18261-2

Note from the publisher:
Please use this product in conjunction with the official specification and sample assessment materials. Ask your teacher if you are unsure where to find them.

Contents

Check your answers on the free revision app or at www.scholastic.co.uk/gcse

How to use this book

This Study Guide is designed to help you prepare effectively for your AQA GCSE English literature exam question on *Romeo and Juliet* (Paper 1, Section A).

The content has been organised in a sequence that builds confidence, and which will deepen your knowledge and understanding of the play step by step. Therefore, it is best to work through this book in the order that it is presented.

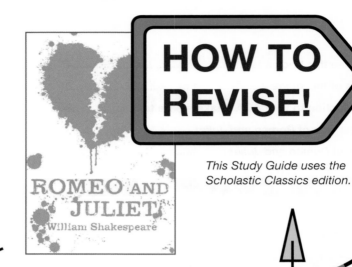

HOW TO REVISE!

This Study Guide uses the Scholastic Classics edition.

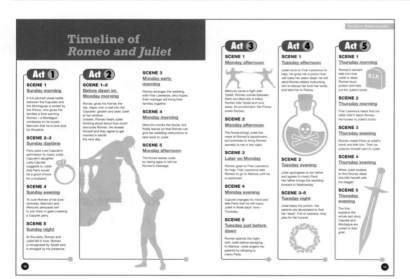

Know the plot

1 It is very important that you know the plot well: to be clear about what happens and in what order. The **timeline** on pages 10–11 provides a useful overview of the plot, highlighting key events.

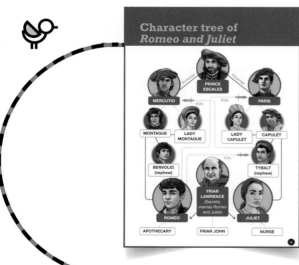

The **character tree** on page 9 introduces you to the main characters of the text.

The chronological section

2 The **chronological section** on pages 12–59 takes you through the play scene by scene, providing plot summaries and pointing out important details. It is also designed to help you think about the structure of the play.

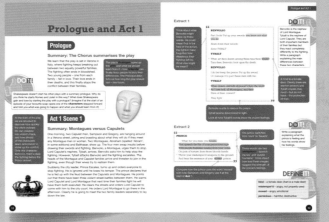

This section provides an in-depth exploration of themes or character development, drawing your attention to how Shakespeare's language choices reveal the play's meaning.

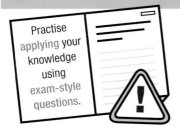

Practise applying your knowledge using exam-style questions.

The play as a whole

3 The second half of the guide is retrospective: it helps you to look back over the whole play through a number of relevant 'lenses': characters, themes, Shakespeare's language, verse forms and structural features.

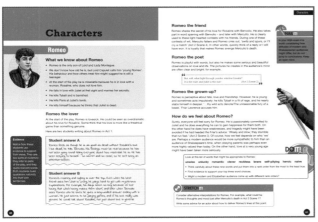

Doing well in your AQA Exam

Stick to the **TIME LIMITS** you will need to in the exam.

4 Finally, you will find an extended 'Doing well in your AQA exam' section which guides you through the process of understanding questions, and planning and writing answers.

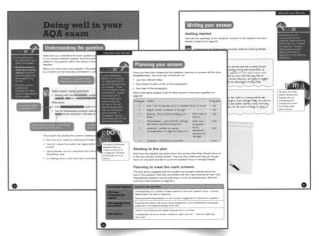

Features of this guide

The best way to retain information is to take an active approach to revision.

Throughout this book, you will find lots of features that will make your revision an active, successful process.

SNAPIT!

Use the Snap it! feature in the revision app to take pictures of key concepts and information. Great for revision on the go!

DEFINEIT!

Explains the meaning of difficult words from the set texts.

Callouts Additional explanations of important points.

words shown in **purple bold** can be found in the glossary on pages 94–95

Find methods of relaxation that work for you throughout the revision period.

Regular exercise helps stimulate the brain and will help you relax.

DOIT!

Activities to embed your knowledge and understanding and prepare you for the exams.

NAILIT!

Succinct and vital tips on how to do well in your exam.

STRETCHIT!

Provides content that stretches you further.

REVIEW IT!

Helps you to consolidate and understand what you have learned before moving on.

Revise in pairs or small groups and deliver presentations on topics to each other.

FOR HIGH-MARK QUESTIONS, SPEND TIME **PLANNING** YOUR ANSWER!

AQA exam-style question

AQA exam-style sample questions based on the extract shown are given on some pages. Use the sample mark scheme on page 85 to help you assess your responses. This will also help you understand what you could do to improve your response.

FREE REVISION APP

- The **free revision app** can be downloaded to your mobile phone (iOS and Android), making **on the go revision** easy.

- Use the revision calendar to help map out your revision in the lead-up to the exam.

- Complete multiple-choice questions and create your own SNAP**IT!** revision cards.

  www.scholastic.co.uk/gcse

Online answers and additional resources

All of the tasks in this book are designed to get you thinking and to consolidate your understanding through thought and application. Therefore, it is important to write your own answers before checking. Some questions include tables where you need to fill in your answer in the book. Other questions require you to use a separate piece of paper so that you can draft your response and work out the best way of answering.

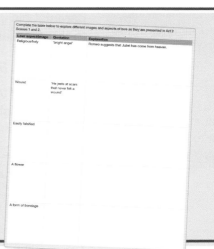

Get plenty of sleep, especially the night before an exam.

LOOK AFTER YOURSELF

Help your brain by looking after your whole body!

Once you have worked through a section, you can check your answers to Do it!, Stretch it!, Review it! and the exam practice sections on the app or at **www.scholastic.co.uk/gcse**.

Why study *Romeo and Juliet*?

Although *Romeo and Juliet* was written more than 400 years ago, it has kept its appeal for modern audiences. The subject matter of the play still has a strong immediate relevance. Two teenagers – Romeo and Juliet – come from rival families that have been feuding and fighting for a long time. The teenagers fall in love at first sight. They are forced to keep their relationship secret, not just because they are from opposing families, but also because the girl's parents have arranged a marriage for her. The secrecy of the teenagers' relationship creates an intense commitment between the two of them resulting in tragedy.

How many modern teenagers have kept a relationship secret to avoid their parents' disapproval? The plot of *Romeo and Juliet* gives powerful expression to this familiar experience.

Romeo and Juliet in your AQA exam

Romeo and Juliet is examined in Section A (the first half) of the first AQA GCSE English Literature exam, Paper 1: Shakespeare and the 19th-century novel. Here is how it fits into the overall assessment framework:

Paper 1 Time: **1 hour 45 minutes**	Paper 2 Time: **2 hours 15 minutes**
Section A: Shakespeare: *Romeo and Juliet*	Section A: Modern prose or drama
Section B: 19th-century novel	Section B: Poetry anthology
	Section C: Unseen poetry

There will be just one question on *Romeo and Juliet* and you should not answer questions on any other Shakespeare play. Just answer the *Romeo and Juliet* question. You should spend 55 minutes planning and writing your answer to the question. There are 30 marks available for the Shakespeare question, plus four extra marks for good vocabulary, spelling, sentences and punctuation (VSSP, sometimes called 'SPaG').

The Shakespeare question will come with a short extract from the play printed on the exam paper. You will find the question straight after the extract. The question will focus on character and/or theme. You must answer the question in relation to the extract and to relevant other parts of the play that you have chosen.

A character tree

The 'character tree' on page 9 should help you to fix in your mind the names of the characters, their relationships and who did what to whom.

Timeline of *Romeo and Juliet*

The timeline on pages 10–11 provides a visual overview of the plot, highlighting key events which take place over the course of the play. It will also help you to think about the structure of the play.

NAILIT!

- Keep a close watch on the time in the exam. Don't spend more than 55 minutes on the Shakespeare: *Romeo and Juliet* question or you will have less time to write your answer to the 19th-century novel question in Section B.

- Take special care over spelling, punctuation and grammar as there are four extra marks available for these.

Character tree of *Romeo and Juliet*

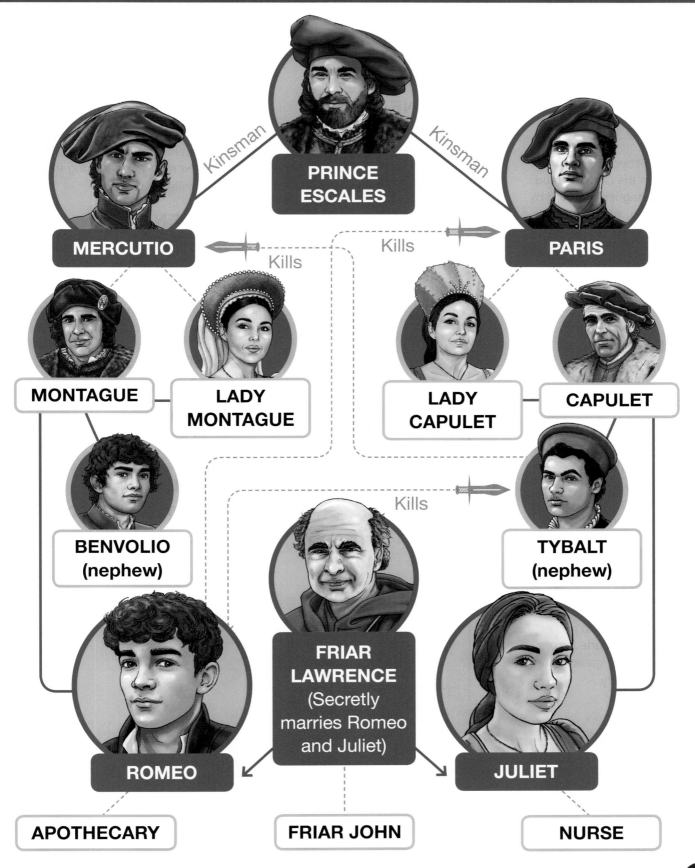

PRINCE ESCALES

Kinsman — MERCUTIO

Kinsman — PARIS

Kills → MERCUTIO

Kills → PARIS

MONTAGUE — LADY MONTAGUE

LADY CAPULET — CAPULET

BENVOLIO (nephew)

TYBALT (nephew)

Kills → TYBALT

FRIAR LAWRENCE (Secretly marries Romeo and Juliet)

ROMEO

JULIET

APOTHECARY

FRIAR JOHN

NURSE

Timeline of *Romeo and Juliet*

Act 1

SCENE 1
Sunday morning

A full-pitched street battle between the Capulets and the Montagues is ended by the Prince, who gives the families a final warning.

Romeo – a Montague - confesses to his cousin Benvolio that he is lovesick for Rosaline.

SCENE 2–3
Sunday daytime

Paris asks Lord Capulet's permission to marry Juliet, Capulet's daughter. Lady Capulet suggests to Juliet that Paris would be a good choice for a husband.

SCENE 4
Sunday evening

To cure Romeo of his love-sickness, Benvolio and Mercutio persuade him to join them in gatecrashing a Capulet party.

SCENE 5
Sunday night

At the party, Romeo and Juliet fall in love. Romeo is recognised by Tybalt who is enraged by his presence.

Act 2

SCENE 1–2
Before dawn on Monday morning

Romeo gives his friends the slip, leaps over a wall into the Capulets' garden and sees Juliet at her window.
Unseen, Romeo hears Juliet thinking aloud about how much she loves Romeo. He reveals himself and they agree to get married in secret the next day.

SCENE 3
Monday early morning

Romeo arranges the wedding with Friar Lawrence, who hopes their marriage will bring their families together.

SCENE 4
Monday morning

Mercutio mocks the Nurse, but finally leaves so that Romeo can give her wedding instructions to take back to Juliet.

SCENE 5
Monday afternoon

The Nurse teases Juliet by taking ages to tell her Romeo's message.

SCENE 6
Monday afternoon

Romeo and Juliet meet Friar Lawrence for their secret wedding.

Act 3

SCENE 1
Monday afternoon

Mercutio picks a fight with Tybalt. Romeo comes between them but Mercutio is killed. Romeo kills Tybalt and runs away. As punishment, the Prince exiles Romeo.

SCENE 2
Monday afternoon

The Nurse brings Juliet the news of Romeo's banishment, but promises to bring Romeo secretly to her in the night.

SCENE 3
Later on Monday

Romeo goes to Friar Lawrence for help. Friar Lawrence tells Romeo to go to Mantua until he is pardoned.

SCENE 4
Monday evening

Capulet changes his mind and tells Paris that he will marry Juliet in three days' time – Thursday.

SCENE 5
Tuesday just before dawn

Romeo spends the night with Juliet before escaping to Mantua. Juliet angers her parents by refusing to marry Paris.

Act 4

SCENE 1
Tuesday afternoon

Juliet turns to Friar Lawrence for help. He gives her a potion that will make her seem dead. He will send Romeo letters instructing him to rescue her from her tomb, and take her to Padua.

SCENE 2
Tuesday evening

Juliet apologises to her father and agrees to marry Paris. Her father brings the wedding forward to Wednesday.

SCENE 3–5
Tuesday night

Juliet takes the potion. Her parents are devastated to find her 'dead'. Full of sadness, they plan for her funeral.

Act 5

SCENE 1
Thursday morning

Romeo's servant tells him that Juliet is dead. Romeo buys poison and sets out for Juliet's tomb.

SCENE 2
Thursday morning

Friar Lawrence hears that his letter didn't reach Romeo. He hurries to Juliet's tomb.

SCENE 3
Thursday evening

Romeo meets Paris at Juliet's tomb and kills him. Then he poisons himself next to Juliet.

When Juliet awakes to find Romeo dead she kills herself with his dagger.

The friar explains the whole sad story. Capulet and Montague are united in their grief.

Prologue

Summary: The Chorus summarises the play

We learn that the play is set in Verona in Italy, where fighting keeps breaking out between two equally powerful families. The fighting often ends in bloodshed. Two young people – one from each family – fall in love. Their love ends in their deaths, and this finally stops the conflict between their families.

The play's **Prologue** sums up the **plot** and what we should learn from it – how **tragedy** can finally force people to bury their differences. The Prologue even tells us how long the play should last – two hours.

DOIT!

Shakespeare doesn't start his other plays with a summary prologue. Why do you think he starts *Romeo and Juliet* in this way? What does Shakespeare gain and lose by starting the play with a prologue? (Imagine if at the start of an episode of your favourite soap opera one of the **characters** stepped forward and told you what was going to happen and what you should learn from it!)

At the start of the play we are shocked to discover how quickly the city's ordinary life can collapse into violent chaos, and how almost all the characters seem determined to stoke up the conflict. Only one character, Benvolio, tried to stop the fighting before the Prince arrived.

Act 1 Scene 1

Summary: Montagues versus Capulets

One morning, two Capulet men, Sampson and Gregory, are hanging around in a Verona street, joking and boasting about what they will do if they meet any Montague men or women. Two Montagues, Abraham (spelled 'Abram', in some editions) and Balthasar, show up. The four men swap insults before drawing their swords and fighting. Benvolio, a Montague, urges them to stop. Lord Capulet's nephew, Tybalt, arrives. Benvolio asks him to help stop the fighting. However, Tybalt attacks Benvolio and the fighting escalates. The heads of the Montague and Capulet families arrive and threaten to join in the fighting, even though their wives try to restrain them.

Suddenly the city leader, Prince Escales, turns up and orders everyone to stop fighting. He is ignored until he loses his temper. The prince declares that he is fed up with the feud between the Capulets and Montagues. He points out that there have been three violent street-battles between them. He warns Lord Capulet and Lord Montague that next time their families fight he will have them both executed. He clears the streets and orders Lord Capulet to come with him to the city court. He orders Lord Montague to go there in the afternoon. Clearly he is going to meet the two family leaders separately to lay down the law.

Extract 1

Think about what Benvolio might mean by these words. He could mean that in the heat of the action, the fighters have forgotten how disastrous their fighting will be. What else might he mean?

DO IT!

Benvolio is the nephew of Lord Montague. Tybalt is the nephew of Lord Capulet. They are both important members of their families but they react completely differently to the fighting. Write a paragraph explaining the main differences between these two characters.

> **BENVOLIO**
>
> Part, fools! Put up your swords, you know not what you do.
>
> *Beats down their swords*
>
> *Enter TYBALT*
>
> **TYBALT**
>
> 5 What, art thou drawn among these heartless hinds?
> Turn thee, Benvolio, look upon thy death.
>
> **BENVOLIO**
>
> I do but keep the peace. Put up thy sword,
> Or manage it to part these men with me.
>
> **TYBALT**
>
> What, drawn, and talk of peace? I hate the word,
> 10 As I hate hell, all Montagues, and thee.
> Have at thee, coward!
>
> *They fight*

A hind is a female deer. Clearly there are women present and Tybalt implies they need – but do not have – the protection of men.

Benvolio wants to restore the peace.

Tybalt seems determined to fight.

Look at how Tybalt's words show his violent feelings.

Extract 2

> **PRINCE**
>
> … What, ho! you men, you beasts,
> That quench the fire of your pernicious rage
> With purple fountains issuing from your veins,
> On pain of torture, from those bloody hands
> 5 Throw your mistemper'd weapons to the ground,
> And hear the sentence of your moved prince.

The prince switches from 'men' to 'beasts'.

These words use two **metaphors**: 'quench the fire' and 'purple fountains'. Think about how well these images suggest the strength of the prince's feelings.

Compare how the prince uses the word 'moved' with how Sampson and Gregory use it at the start of **Act** 1.

DO IT!

Write a paragraph explaining what the prince is feeling and how his words show his feelings.

DEFINE IT!

hind – a female deer; (hart is a male deer)

mistemper'd – angry, not properly used

moved – angry, emotional

pernicious – harmful, destructive

Act 1 Scene 2

Summary: '…woo her, gentle Paris, get her heart'

Capulet tells Paris that it shouldn't be hard for him and Montague 'to keep the peace'. Paris asks Capulet's permission to marry Juliet, Capulet's only remaining child. Capulet asks Paris to wait a couple of years. Paris replies that girls younger than Juliet are already 'happy mothers'. Capulet protests that girls are 'marred' (damaged) by such young motherhood. He allows Paris to 'woo' Juliet and to come to his feast to compare her favourably with other girls there, but he insists that he will allow Juliet to make her own choice of husband.

Capulet gives Peter, his servant, a guest list for his feast, but Peter cannot read and asks Romeo to read it for him. Benvolio tells Romeo that they should go so that Romeo can compare Rosaline with more beautiful girls. Outraged, Romeo only agrees to go to the feast to admire Rosaline.

Capulet the father

At this point in the play, Lord Capulet seems loving and protective towards his daughter. He even says that Juliet will be allowed to decide her own future: deciding who she marries and when will be in 'her scope of choice'. Capulet will give her his 'according voice' – his agreement.

DO IT!

Re-read from the beginning of Scene 2 to 'My house and welcome on their pleasure stay'. Which of the following statements do you think is *most* true? Explain your choice by referring to evidence in this part of the play only.

- Capulet is very protective towards Juliet.
- Capulet loves Juliet and depends on her.
- Capulet wants Paris to marry Juliet.
- Paris is a paedophile.

Extract 1

In this speech, Romeo's choice of **language** makes his love into a sort of religion with Rosaline as a goddess.

STRETCH IT!

To get the highest marks in your AQA exam, you need to explore detailed links between different parts of the play. Compare how Romeo links love and religion in his speech in extract 1 here with how Romeo and Juliet do something similar at their first meeting (Act 1 Scene 5). Why do you think Shakespeare makes this connection between love and religion?

Notice how Romeo presents his love in religious terms: it would be heresy to consider not loving Rosaline.

The falsehood (lie) is the idea that anyone could be more beautiful than Rosaline.

> **ROMEO**
>
> When the devout religion of mine eye
> Maintains such falsehood, then turn tears to fire;
> And these, who often drown'd could never die,
> Transparent heretics, be burnt for liars.
> 5 One fairer than my love? The all-seeing sun
> Ne'er saw her match since first the world begun.

Act 1 Scene 3

Summary: 'How stands your disposition to be married?'

We learn that Juliet is nearly 14. The Nurse recalls embarrassing details from Juliet's early childhood until Lady Capulet stops her. Then Lady Capulet asks Juliet how she might feel about marrying Paris, pointing out that many Verona 'ladies' of her age 'are…already mothers.'

Lady Capulet informs Juliet that she had her when she was about Juliet's current age. The Nurse and Lady Capulet praise Paris's virtues and attractions. Lady Capulet calls Paris a 'precious book of love' that needs Juliet as its cover. Juliet agrees to consider Paris as a husband. The Nurse encourages her to look forward to her wedding night.

DO IT!

What might Juliet be thinking and feeling about what her mother says? Write Juliet's diary entry. Use what you know about Juliet to imagine her thoughts and feelings.

Extract 2

Here Lady Capulet uses an extended metaphor in which Paris is a book and Juliet is the book's cover. The highlighted words and phrases are part of the extended metaphor.

> **LADY CAPULET**
> Read o'er the volume of young Paris' face,
> And find delight writ there with beauty's pen;
> Examine every married lineament,
> And see how one another lends content,
> 5 And what obscured in this fair volume lies
> Find written in the margent of his eyes.
> This precious book of love, this unbound lover,
> To beautify him, only lacks a cover:
> The fish lives in the sea; and 'tis much pride
> 10 For fair without the fair within to hide:
> That book in many's eyes doth share the glory,
> That in gold clasps locks in the golden story;
> So shall you share all that he doth possess,
> By having him, making yourself no less.

In this image Juliet completes Paris by being a beautiful cover for him. Her beauty will suggest that he is equally wonderful.

She won't lose anything by being Paris's wife (although he will be the 'golden story' while she will only be the 'gold clasps').

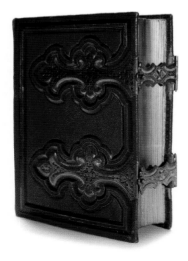

DEFINE IT!

devout – sincere, completely committed

heretic – a person who rejects official religious teaching; centuries ago some heretics were executed for their 'heresy', sometimes by drowning or burning

margent – margin

obscured – hidden

writ – written

Act 1 Scene 4

Summary: On the way to the Capulet feast

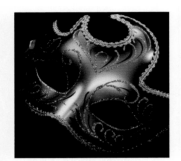

Romeo, Benvolio and Mercutio arrive in disguise at the Capulets' house. Benvolio intends to enter, dance and leave. Romeo claims he is too weighed down by his 'soul of lead' to dance: he will just carry the torch. Mercutio tells Romeo to 'beat love down' and enjoy himself. Romeo will not be cheered up. Mercutio describes a dream he has had about a tiny fairy called Queen Mab who makes people dream of their desires. For example, soldiers dream of battles; lawyers dream of fees; lovers dream of love. (The Queen Mab speech is typical of Mercutio. It shows his energy, wit and imagination and how much he enjoys teasing others.)

Romeo suddenly stops Mercutio, accusing him of talking 'of nothing'. Mercutio agrees but points out that dreams come out of a 'vain fantasy', probably implying that Romeo's lovesickness has no more worth or 'substance' than a dream.

Benvolio urges them to get moving or else they are going to miss the party. Romeo agrees, but he also has a premonition of his own 'untimely death' as a result of 'this night's revels'. (Romeo already predicts tragedy.)

DO IT!

Think about *Romeo and Juliet* and about any other romances you have read or watched. Do those stories hint at the sort of ending they will have – sad or happy? Do you like to predict endings? Is it disappointing if a story turns out as expected?

STRETCH IT!

Actors play Mercutio in this scene in different ways. For example, some actors suggest that Mercutio has almost gone mad and Romeo has to hush and calm him. What different ways could Mercutio be played here? Briefly explain your ideas.

Fate and foreshadowing

Romeo and Juliet is both a romance and a tragedy. Perhaps it makes the story even more romantic that a shadow of doom hangs over the lovers right from the beginning. The Prologue warns us that they are 'star-cross'd', suggesting the idea that our fate is 'in the stars' and there's nothing we can do to change it. To emphasise the inevitability of disaster, we are told that Romeo and Juliet's love is 'death-mark'd'. Romeo senses his terrible fate even before he meets Juliet, just as he is about to go into the Capulet feast:

> …my mind misgives
> Some consequence yet hanging in
> the stars…

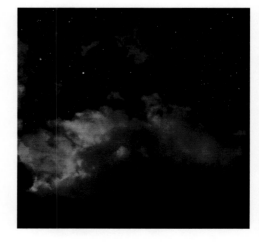

The audience's sense that the story is going to have a tragic ending helps keep their attention throughout. In other words, **foreshadowing** the ending is one of Shakespeare's ways of creating tension and a sense of the inevitability of tragedy.

Extract 1

Here we see the clear difference between Mercutio's and Romeo's attitudes to love. Mercutio and Romeo speak in poetry (or '**verse**'). This gives their speeches an elegance that makes their ideas neat and gives them authority: in other words, the poetry is used for **effect**.

> **MERCUTIO**
> You are a lover, borrow Cupid's wings,
> And soar with them above a common bound.
>
> **ROMEO**
> I am too sore enpierced with his shaft
> To soar with his light feathers, and so bound
> 5 I cannot bound a pitch above dull woe.
> Under love's heavy burden do I sink.
>
> **MERCUTIO**
> And to sink in it should you burden love,
> Too great oppression for a tender thing.
>
> **ROMEO**
> Is love a tender thing? it is too rough,
> 10 Too rude, too boist'rous, and it pricks like thorn.
>
> **MERCUTIO**
> If love be rough with you, be rough with love:
> Prick love for pricking, and you beat love down.

Romeo's words present him as a victim of love, suffering physical pain.

By contrast, Mercutio sees love as something to be challenged and overpowered. Of course, the two characters might be thinking of different things when they use the word 'love'. Mercutio's first line here is a perfect example of an **iambic pentameter**.

Extract 2

> **ROMEO**
> I fear, too early: for my mind misgives
> Some consequence yet hanging in the stars,
> Shall bitterly begin his fearful date
> With this night's revels; and expire the term
> 5 Of a despised life closed in my breast,
> By some vile forfeit of untimely death.
> But he that hath the steerage of my course
> Direct my sail! On, lusty gentlemen.

In Shakespeare's time – and now – many people believed that the stars somehow controlled or foretold their fate.

What does Romeo mean by 'a despised life'? Perhaps he hates his own life, or perhaps he senses that Fate hates him.

'Forfeit' suggests that Romeo expects to be punished. What has he done (or is about to do) that might deserve punishment?

DO IT!

So far, to what extent has Shakespeare set Romeo up as a *victim*?

Briefly explain your views by referring to evidence in the **script**.

DEFINE IT!

Cupid – in ancient mythology, Cupid was the god of desire; he was often portrayed blindfolded; he fired arrows from his bow and whoever was hit would immediately fall in love

enpierced – stabbed, pierced

misgive – to experience fear or apprehension about the future

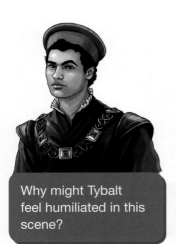

Act 1 Scene 5

Summary: The Capulet feast

Capulet's servants frantically clear a space for the dancing. Capulet welcomes his masked visitors and urges the women to dance with them. He regrets that he is too old for dancing.

Romeo sees Juliet and forgets Rosaline instantly 'I ne'er saw true beauty till this night.' (In the previous scene Romeo said it would be heresy to prefer any woman to Rosaline.)

Realising Romeo is a Montague, Tybalt sends for his sword. However, his uncle Capulet tells Tybalt that Romeo has a good reputation and to 'let him alone'. When Tybalt protests, Capulet angrily threatens him with punishment. Tybalt fumes with resentment for Romeo.

Romeo and Juliet exchange their love for each other in terms that make it sound like a religious ceremony. (Look carefully at the religious words Romeo and Juliet use to define their feelings of love.) They kiss. Juliet is called away by her mother and the Nurse tells Romeo who Juliet is. Romeo is shocked that he is in love with a Capulet.

Capulet ends the evening. Juliet sends the Nurse to find out Romeo's name, saying that if he is married, she will have to die unmarried. (Juliet doesn't just fall in love instantly: she also instantly wants to *marry* Romeo.) She is horrified to find that she is in love with 'a loathed enemy'.

The **Chorus** sums up the situation that Romeo and Juliet find themselves in.

> Why might Tybalt feel humiliated in this scene?

Tybalt

Here is part of what a student wrote about Tybalt. An examiner's notes are next to the student's answer.

Earlier in Act 1 we discovered that Tybalt hates all Montagues and will attack them whenever he meets them. Because of that we worry that Romeo is now in real danger. Tybalt's hatred will have been made worse by being humiliated by Romeo and his uncle. He is so overwhelmed with feeling that he feels his 'flesh tremble' and he only leaves Romeo alone because he has to. His feelings have left him full of 'bitterest gall'.	Useful, relevant reference to other part of play. Direct references (quotations) used neatly and effectively to back up point about why Tybalt is so dangerous.

Write another paragraph about Tybalt exploring how his behaviour in Act 3 Scene 1 (when he fights Mercutio and Romeo) might be explained by events in Act 1.

STRETCHIT!

Explain how Tybalt's attitudes and values might affect his feelings at this point in the play. For example, you might consider his attitude towards women and manliness.

Extract 1

"

ROMEO

[*To JULIET*] If I profane with my unworthiest hand
This holy shrine, the gentle sin is this,
My lips, two blushing pilgrims, ready stand
To smooth that rough touch with a tender kiss.

JULIET

5 Good pilgrim, you do wrong your hand too much,
Which mannerly devotion shows in this,
For saints have hands that pilgrims' hands do touch,
And palm to palm is holy palmers' kiss.

ROMEO

Have not saints lips, and holy palmers too?

JULIET

10 Ay, pilgrim, lips that they must use in prayer.

ROMEO

O then, dear saint, let lips do what hands do:
They pray, grant thou, lest faith turn to despair.

JULIET

Saints do not move, though grant for prayers' sake.

ROMEO

Then move not while my prayer's effect I take.
15 Thus from my lips, by thine, my sin is purg'd.

JULIET

Then have my lips the sin that they have took.

ROMEO

Sin from my lips? O trespass sweetly urg'd!
Give me my sin again.

"

Romeo says that if he has disrespected this shrine to love (Juliet) by touching her, then he will compensate by committing a gentler sin – smoothing the 'rough touch' with a kiss.

Romeo begins an extended metaphor of love as holy. Juliet joins in.

Both of them speak in lines that rhyme every other line. Sometimes they even finish each other's rhymes, thus emphasising the lovers' unity.

DEFINE IT!

palmer – a Christian pilgrim returning from the holy land carrying a palm

pilgrim – someone who makes a special and respectful journey to a holy place

profane – to treat a religious matter disrespectfully

shrine – a holy place

trespass – sin

Romeo and Juliet are 'chatting each other up' without the normal parental approval. Perhaps presenting their love as a sort of prayer excuses them for being so forward with each other.

The poetry's even, iambic lines emphasise the lovers' entrancement – it's as though they have hypnotised each other.

AQA exam-style question

Starting with this conversation in extract 1 above, how does Shakespeare present Romeo and Juliet's attitudes towards romantic love in *Romeo and Juliet?*

Write about:

- how Shakespeare presents Romeo and Juliet's attitudes towards romantic love in this conversation

- how Shakespeare presents Romeo and Juliet's attitudes towards romantic love in the play as a whole.

[30 marks]

Character and theme essentials

Romeo

Romeo is the son of Lord Montague. He describes himself as 'sick' with love. He is very sad because Rosaline doesn't love him. He says he will never be able to forget her: when he looks at other women they only remind him of Rosaline's perfection. Yet the moment he sees Juliet he forgets Rosaline: 'I ne'er saw true beauty till this night' (Act 1 Scene 5). Perhaps Romeo is fickle in his feelings and over-dramatic about them.

Juliet

Juliet is the Capulets' only surviving child. Although she is only 13, in Verona she already counts as a woman. She falls in love with Romeo as soon as she meets him. The rich and powerful young man, Paris, wants to marry her, but she would rather die than marry anyone but Romeo ('My only love' – Act 1 Scene 5). She seems very grown up despite her youth: she handles her mother with respect and tact, and she matches Romeo's clever speeches.

Mercutio

Mercutio is neither a Montague nor a Capulet. (We later discover that he is related to the Prince and to Paris.) Mercutio believes in enjoying life and not giving in to sadness: 'If love be rough with you, be rough with love' (Act 1 Scene 4). He loves playing with words.

The Nurse

The Nurse has been like a mother to Juliet since she was a baby. She even fed Juliet from her own breast. She talks at length, repeating herself and taking ages to get to the point. She often interrupts, sometimes with bawdy references such as 'Women grow by men' (Act 1 Scene 3), meaning that men make women pregnant. The Nurse is a loyal servant. Although she is over-talkative and embarrassing, Juliet and her mother clearly love her and rely on her.

Benvolio

Benvolio is Romeo's cousin and friend. He tries to stop the street fighting, but seems proud of how he fought Tybalt ('hiss'd him in scorn' – Act 1 Scene 1). He offers to help Montague find out what is wrong with Romeo. He seems generous and unselfish but perhaps he is a busybody. There are different ways that Benvolio could be **interpreted**. He tries to keep the peace, but he does fight Tybalt, and his report of the fight could sound boastful.

Love

In Act 1 we are introduced to passionate (and sometimes painful) romantic love. Benvolio notes that for Romeo love is 'tyrannous and rough' (Act 1 Scene 1). Romeo describes love as 'madness' (Act 1 Scene 1), a poison – 'gall' – that has made him 'ill'. Juliet and Romeo treat love as something holy. We also see love as bonds of duty and affection within families and between friends.

NAILIT!

In your AQA exam, to get the highest marks you should consider different interpretations of characters rather than making simple judgements about them. A good way to do that is to think about the choices an actor could make when playing a character.

Conflict

Shakespeare presents the conflict between the Montagues and Capulets as ridiculous, destructive and pointless. Sampson and Gregory provoke the fight and the Montagues accept the provocation willingly, almost as though provocation and skirmishing is a routine ritual. Tybalt's hatred for the Montagues is excessive, but he throws it enthusiastically into the battle – like oil on flames. The Prince is exasperated.

Fate

We know that the story will end in tragedy: the Prologue tells us, and so we are always aware that Romeo and Juliet cannot escape their terrible fate whatever they do. As Romeo is about to enter the Capulets' house he gets the feeling that the night will lead to his 'untimely death' (Act 1 Scene 4), and at the end of the party Juliet half-predicts her own death: if Romeo is already married 'My grave is like to be my wedding-bed' (Act 1 Scene 5).

DEFINE IT!

bawdy – humorous sexual references

REVIEW IT!

1. The Shakespeare exam question is on Paper 1. Is it section A or section B?
2. How long should you spend on the Shakespeare question?
3. Why does Sampson tell the Capulets that he bites his thumb but not *at them*?
4. What does the Prince threaten if there are any more street battles?
5. Why is Romeo sad at the start of the play?
6. What does Romeo mean by the use of the **oxymorons** 'brawling love' and 'loving hate'?
7. What is Benvolio's plan to get Romeo to forget the woman he loves?
8. How does Capulet react to Paris's request to marry Juliet?
9. What does the Nurse's use of the metaphor, 'a man of wax', suggest about Paris?
10. What does Romeo fear just before he goes into the Capulet party?
11. Romeo is in disguise at the party, so how does Tybalt recognise him as a Montague?
12. Why doesn't Tybalt throw Romeo out of the party?
13. What does Tybalt say will happen because he has had to leave Romeo alone?
14. What reward does the Nurse suggest will come to the man who marries Juliet?
15. What does Juliet fear will happen if Romeo turns out to be married?
16. How many brothers does Romeo have?
17. Look at the first meeting of Romeo and Juliet. Write down eight words and/or short phrases that present their feelings as religious and holy.
18. How much do Juliet's parents love her? Give reasons for your thoughts.
19. Romeo says:

> Is love a tender thing? It is too rough,
> Too rude, too boisterous, and it pricks like thorn. (Act 1 Scene 4)

What does he mean?

20. Explain why Romeo and Juliet might have fallen in love so quickly and deeply.

Act 2

Act 2 Scene 1

Summary: Where art thou, Romeo?

Benvolio and Mercutio are standing next to the Capulets' orchard wall which Benvolio saw Romeo climb over. They call to him but when they get no reply Mercutio makes jokes about conjuring Romeo back to them. In the course of his conjuring he mocks Romeo for his well-known lovesick behaviour. Then he entertains himself with increasingly rude sexual suggestions about Romeo and Rosaline. Finally, Benvolio and Mercutio give up and leave.

STRETCH IT!

Mercutio's version of love is crudely sexual. He mocks romantic love as being all about sighing dramatically, and writing bad poetry with corny rhymes such as 'love' and 'dove'. These were considered typical features of 'courtly love' – love as a sort of art. In the next scene, Romeo defends his own romantic habits by claiming that Mercutio is only scornful because he has never felt the pain of real love: 'He jests at scars that never felt a wound.' Look for other examples of Mercutio's cynicism and scorn.

Act 2 Scene 2

Summary: 'Wherefore art thou, Romeo?'

From the Capulets' orchard, Romeo sees Juliet at an upstairs window. She thinks aloud about Romeo. She despairs that her love is a Montague: 'Wherefore [why] art thou Romeo?' When she says she'd happily take his name by marrying him, she is shocked to hear Romeo's voice, which she recognises. She warns him that her relatives will kill him if they find him there and asks how he found her. He says that he was led by love whose 'light wings' helped him over the high wall.

Embarrassed that he knows her true feelings, Juliet worries that he will think her too easily won. (As a girl, Juliet feels that she should not reveal her feelings for a boy until she is sure about his feelings for her.) She declares that their relationship is 'too rash, too unadvis'd, too sudden' and says goodnight, so Romeo offers his 'love's faithful vow' in exchange for hers. She assures him her love for him is 'infinite'. Romeo promises to make arrangements for their wedding by 9 am, and Juliet says she will send someone to find out the details.

 STRETCH IT!

AQA encourages students to consider how a modern audience might respond to the play. Think about how a modern reader or watcher might respond to Juliet's situation. Should Juliet feel embarrassed about being 'caught out' expressing her true feelings? Would a girl feel the same today as Juliet did then?

DO IT!

Complete the table below to explore different images and aspects of love as they are presented in Act 2 Scenes 1 and 2.

Love aspect/image	Quotation	Explanation
Religious/holy	'bright angel'	Romeo suggests that Juliet has come from heaven.
Wound	'He jests at scars that never felt a wound'	
Easily falsified		
A flower		
A form of bondage		

Romantic love

Love is not presented always as 'a preserving sweet' (Romeo, Act 1 Scene 1): it is often presented in *Romeo and Juliet* as painful and even life-threatening. In the 'balcony scene' love is presented in terms of a variety of images or aspects, for example, religious/holy, a wound, pure, easily falsified, a flower, a form of bondage.

Extract 1

Light and dark is a repeating **motif** in the play. This description of Juliet depends on light/dark contrasts, but with light winning. As the play continues, darkness seems to close in on the two lovers.

> **ROMEO**
> Two of the fairest stars in all the heaven,
> Having some business, do entreat her eyes
> To twinkle in their spheres till they return.
> What if her eyes were there, they in her head?
> 5 The brightness of her cheek would shame those stars,
> As daylight doth a lamp; her eyes in heaven
> Would through the airy region stream so bright
> That birds would sing and think it were not night.

The speech describes Juliet in exaggerated terms – her eyes are brighter than stars, and if stars were literally in her eyes they would be dimmer than the glow from her cheeks.

STRETCH IT!

How might this idea of 'birds would sing and think it were not night' become very meaningful later in the play?

Extract 2

> **JULIET**
> I have no joy of this contract tonight,
> It is too rash, too unadvis'd, too sudden,
> Too like the lightning, which doth cease to be
>
> Ere one can say It lightens. Sweet, good night.
> 5 This bud of love, by summer's ripening breath,
> May prove a beauteous flower when next we meet.

Juliet realises that sudden passionate love might burn itself out like lightning.

She realises that love should not be forced, but instead allowed to ripen like a budding flower.

She hints that they *should* part now and allow their love to develop slowly into something strong and stable, but of course that is not what they do.

STRETCH IT!

Look carefully at what Juliet says here about love and relationships. Why do you think that she does not follow her own advice about allowing love to ripen slowly?

DEFINE IT!

airy region – sky

art – are

entreat – beg

fair – beautiful

thou – you

wherefore – why

Act 2 Scene 3

Summary: Romeo asks Friar Lawrence to marry him to Juliet

Friar Lawrence (spelled 'Laurence' in some editions) marvels that some of the herbs he gathers cure if smelled, but kill if tasted. He realises that people too contain good and evil – until one or the other gets the upper hand.

Friar Lawrence is surprised to see Romeo so early. He suspects that either Romeo is too troubled to sleep in, or he has been up all night. Romeo says he has been feasting with the Capulets but that his visit to the Friar will benefit his enemies as much as himself.

He announces his love for Juliet and asks the Friar to marry them 'today'. Friar Lawrence accuses Romeo of being a fickle and shallow lover. Romeo protests that his and Juliet's love is genuine and mutual/shared.

Friar Lawrence finally agrees to the marriage, hoping it will unite Montagues and Capulets, but he worries about the 'haste' of this wedding, and he advises Romeo to go 'Wisely and slow, they stumble that run fast'.

Friar Lawrence

DEFINE IT!

osier – a small willow tree with long flexible shoots used in basketwork

Friar Lawrence is a wise man. Evidence of this is in his view that those who try to accomplish things too quickly tend to fail, and so it is wise to slow down and be cautious. On the other hand, his shrewd decision to marry Romeo and Juliet secretly in order to bring their families together can be seen as risky, even reckless. He is dedicated to helping others. He is up at dawn to gather medicinal plants. His word 'must' as in 'I must upfill this osier cage of ours' shows his sense of dedication and self-sacrifice. He calls Romeo his 'pupil', and clearly the Friar has already advised Romeo about the folly of his infatuation ('doting') for Rosaline.

Turning point

This short scene is a turning point for a number of reasons. Firstly, it gives special emphasis to the theme of opposites – or internal contradictions – that runs throughout the play (see page 27). Secondly, here we form our first impressions of Friar Lawrence, whose actions will turn out to be critical for how the tragedy develops. Finally, this is a 'pivotal' scene because if Friar Lawrence had made a different decision, the plot would have turned out differently. Deciding to marry Romeo and Juliet in secret is a *fateful decision*.

Choose another pivotal scene in the play that could be seen as a turning point – a scene where decisions or actions have a critical influence on the rest of the play's action. Explain briefly what actions and/or decisions make that scene a turning point.

Extract 1

Friar Lawrence is thinking about how all living things are made up of opposites. He starts by observing the benefits of simple herbs and this leads him to consider how people – like herbs – contain both good and evil, but when evil becomes dominant it destroys the person entirely.

"

FRIAR LAWRENCE

O, mickle is the powerful grace that lies
In plants, herbs, stones, and their true qualities:
For nought so vile, that on the earth doth live,
But to the earth some special good doth give;
5 Nor aught so good but, strain'd from that fair use,
Revolts from true birth, stumbling on abuse.
Virtue itself turns vice being misapplied,
And vice sometimes by action dignified.
Enter ROMEO
Within the infant rind of this small flower
10 Poison hath residence, and medicine power;
For this, being smelt, with that part cheers each part;
Being tasted, slays all senses with the heart.
Two such opposed kings encamp them still
In man as well as herbs – grace and rude will;
15 And where the worser is predominant,
Full soon the canker death eats up that plant.

"

Friar Lawrence praises herbs for their healing properties.

Even apparently disgusting natural things are good for something.

But even good things can do harm when they are used for the wrong purpose.

Good people can do harm if they are misled, just as bad people can sometimes do good things.

DEFINE IT!

aught – anything
canker – cancer
mickle – great
nought – nothing

Finally, he uses plants as a symbol of people who are composed of both 'grace' (goodness/kindness) and 'rude will' (selfish desire). These two forces are so powerful that he presents them metaphorically as 'opposed kings'. One side will always win in the end.

Medicinal plants are often both poisonous (for example, when tasted) and beneficial (for example, when smelled).

DO IT!

---

1 Make a short list of words and phrases that mean roughly the same as 'opposites' or 'contradictions'. This list will help you when writing about this theme in the play. Here is one other word: 'paradox'.

2 Find at least two other parts of the play where opposites and contradictions are discussed by a character or shown in action.

• For each of those two parts, write a paragraph explaining those opposites and their significance in the play.

AQA exam-style question

Starting with extract 1 above, explore how Shakespeare presents opposites in *Romeo and Juliet*.

Write about:

• how Shakespeare presents opposites in this extract

• how Shakespeare presents opposites in the play as a whole.

[30 marks]

Act 2 Scene 4

Summary: Romeo tells the Nurse about the wedding arrangements

Mercutio and Benvolio search for Romeo. Benvolio mentions that Tybalt has probably sent a challenge to Romeo. Mercutio praises Tybalt's duelling skills. Romeo arrives.

Mercutio has a long duel of wits and wordplay with Romeo. Mercutio suggests that Romeo slipped away the previous night to visit a prostitute, and Mercutio's teasing becomes increasingly dominated by sexual meanings. He breaks off his battle of wits to congratulate Romeo for being more like his normal self. Mercutio assumes that Rosaline is still the cause of Romeo's misery and insists that word duelling is 'better…than groaning for love'.

The Nurse arrives with her servant, Peter. Mercutio mocks and torments the Nurse, who asks where she can find Romeo. Romeo introduces himself. Mercutio and Benvolio leave. Romeo promises to follow.

The Nurse condemns Mercutio as disrespectful – a 'scurvy knave'. She condemns Peter for not defending her. Romeo instructs the Nurse to tell Juliet to go to confession that afternoon. He asks the Nurse to wait behind the abbey wall to receive a rope ladder that Romeo will use that night to climb into Juliet's bedroom.

The Nurse sets off to tell Juliet the news.

The Nurse

The Nurse puts on a show of dignity and refinement that she cannot really carry off. She orders Peter around, probably to suggest that she is an important person. She does not recognise when the men are teasing her and accepts their sarcasm as compliments. What makes her amusing to the audience is the **dramatic irony** that they understand what she doesn't, so the audience feels superior to the Nurse.

Mercutio

Mercutio has a negative attitude towards women and love. Is he jealous of Romeo? Perhaps Mercutio wants Romeo all to himself, and does not want to have to share his attention with a girlfriend.

NAILIT!

In your AQA exam, always choose and use evidence carefully so that it is very relevant to the point you want to make.

DOIT!

Here are some words that *could* be used to describe the Nurse at different moments in the play:

clever   loyal   foolish   ridiculous   realistic   trustworthy   untrustworthy   confident

Choose the two words that you think are most true of the Nurse – here or more generally in the play. Find and briefly explain some evidence that supports your choice of each word. Find evidence in this scene and/or in other scenes.

Extract 1

Mercutio is fed up with Romeo's dramatic love 'games' and is delighted that the old Romeo is back. He thinks Romeo has now returned to his real self and his normal habits (messing about with his friends).

> **MERCUTIO**
> Why, is not this better now than groaning for love?
> Now art thou sociable, now art thou Romeo; now art thou what thou art, by art as well as by nature.
> For this drivelling love is like a great natural, that runs
> 5 lolling up and down to hide his bauble in a hole.
>
> **BENVOLIO**
> Stop there, stop there.
>
> **MERCUTIO**
> Thou desirest me to stop in my tale against the hair.

The word 'drivelling' conveys Mercutio's disgust powerfully. He means that Romeo's version of love is just nonsense words, but the sound of the word 'drivel' makes us think also of 'dribble', thus reinforcing the idea that Romeo's words are worthless.

Mercutio quickly switches back to the **pun** duel. Almost all his wit is about sex.

DO IT!

Put Mercutio's words above into your own words to make their meaning clear. Try to explain Mercutio's use of double meanings.

Extract 2

Typically, the Nurse can't stick to one topic: she mentions her mistress and then is about to tell a story from her early childhood before she makes herself mention Paris' attempts to marry Juliet.

> **NURSE**
> Well, sir, my mistress is the sweetest lady. Lord, Lord! When 'twas a little prating thing – O, there is a nobleman in town, one Paris, that would fain lay knife aboard; but she, good soul, had as lief
> 5 see a toad, a very toad, as see him. I anger her sometimes, and tell her that Paris is the properer man, but I'll warrant you, when I say so, she looks as pale as any clout in the versal world. Doth not rosemary and Romeo begin both with a letter?

She says she recommends Paris to Juliet sometimes, but this makes Juliet go pale (probably with anger) and this confirms that Juliet has no interest in him.

The Nurse makes a feeble attempt to suggest she too is educated.

Prose and social class

In these two extracts Shakespeare writes not in poetry, but in **prose**. It is likely that he did not think that the elegance of verse was appropriate for Mercutio's crude double meanings, or for the Nurse who is from a lower social class.

DEFINE IT!

bauble – a brightly painted jester's stick

clout – wash rag

confession – a religious routine in which someone confesses their sins to the priest

drivel – words that mean nothing

lief – willingly

natural – idiot

prating – prattling; talking on and on aimlessly

rosemary – a herb often used in cooking

versal – universe (the whole world)

DO IT!

Romeo decided to jump over the orchard wall which put him in immediate danger as shown by Juliet's line, 'If they do see thee, they will murder thee.' Find other actions and/or decisions made by younger characters in the play that have unfortunate consequences and provide a quotation as evidence of this.

Act 2 Scene 5

Summary: 'Unwieldy, slow, heavy and pale as lead'

Juliet waits impatiently for the Nurse to return with news from Romeo. She blames the Nurse's old age for the length of her absence: not only are 'old folks…/Unwieldy, slow, heavy', they also don't understand the urgency of love because they lack 'affections and warm youthful blood'.

At last the Nurse arrives, but instead of giving Juliet her news, she keeps stalling, changing subject and complaining of tiredness and aches. She even suggests that Romeo is a bad choice because he is too full of virtues, both physical and social! (Note how the Nurse teases Juliet by withholding the information she knows Juliet is desperate for. Or is there another explanation?)

Finally, Juliet has to appease the Nurse by massaging her back, apologising and flattering her. The Nurse instructs Juliet to meet Romeo at Friar Lawrence's cell where she will become Romeo's wife. The Nurse then makes some bawdy innuendos about how Juliet will have to take Romeo's burden that night when she is lying under him.

The impatience of youth

The Nurse protests, 'what haste!' and 'Are you so hot' (impatient)? In Act 2 Scene 6, the Friar warns Romeo about the haste of his marriage: 'Too swift arrives as tardy as too slow.'

Juliet shows her intelligence and independence by refusing to play Romeo's word game of putting their love into beautiful words which are just an 'ornament'.

Act 2 Scene 6

Summary: Romeo and Juliet meet for their secret wedding

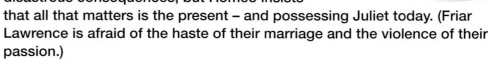

Friar Lawrence fears the wedding might have disastrous consequences, but Romeo insists that all that matters is the present – and possessing Juliet today. (Friar Lawrence is afraid of the haste of their marriage and the violence of their passion.)

Juliet arrives and Friar Lawrence tells her that both he and Romeo should be grateful to her. Romeo invites Juliet to express their joint happiness, but Juliet says her happiness is too great for words, and that people who can measure their good fortune in words are so poor that they are 'beggars'. She is so rich in love that she cannot measure it in mere words.

Friar Lawrence takes them away to marry them.

DO IT!

Explain why both Romeo and Friar Lawrence should be grateful to Juliet.

Extract 1

Here there is a sharp difference between the attitudes of Friar Lawrence and Romeo: Friar Lawrence is paying attention to the future when the consequences of their actions will become apparent; Romeo is only concerned with the present.

FRIAR LAWRENCE
So smile the heavens upon this holy act,
That after-hours with sorrow chide us not.
ROMEO
Amen, amen, but come what sorrow can,
It cannot countervail the exchange of joy
5 That one short minute gives me in her sight.
Do thou but close our hands with holy words,
Then love-devouring death do what he dare,
It is enough I may but call her mine.
FRIAR LAWRENCE
These violent delights have violent ends,
10 And in their triumph die; like fire and powder,
Which as they kiss consume. The sweetest honey
Is loathsome in his own deliciousness,
And in the taste confounds the appetite.
Therefore love moderately: long love doth so;
15 Too swift arrives as tardy as too slow.

Fittingly for a priest, these words sound like a prayer, as though he is calling on God for support. He fears that 'sorrow' will be their punishment. The audience knows that it will.

Romeo's 'amen' response pays respect to the holy aspect of a wedding, but…

…Romeo would trade the whole of the rest of his life for one more minute with Juliet.

Romeo almost dares death to destroy his love. 'Devouring' is a powerful image of Death eating his love greedily and violently.

This idea of death and violence is picked up by Friar Lawrence. He fears Romeo's idea that his triumph in love could lead to destruction. Fire and (gun) powder complement each other but should be kept apart because 'they kiss' (love) and consume each other (kill) at the same moment.

DEFINE IT!

chide – tell off, reproach

confounds – ruins

countervail – equal

DO IT!

Explain what Romeo means by the metaphor 'love-devouring death'.

Explain how death could be said to 'devour' love in one other part of the play.

AQA exam-style question

Starting with this conversation in extract 1 above, explore how Shakespeare presents a connection between love and death in *Romeo and Juliet*.

Write about:

- how Shakespeare presents a connection between love and death in this conversation

- how Shakespeare presents a connection between love and death in the play as a whole.

[30 marks]

NAIL IT!

In your AQA exam, make sure you closely examine the effects of at least two examples of Shakespeare's choice of language.

Choose examples from the extract.

Character and theme essentials

Juliet and Romeo

In this Act – in the space of only a few hours – Juliet and Romeo meet for the first time on their own, decide to marry and then meet Friar Lawrence for their secret wedding. For the audience there are two important questions:

1   What is it about Romeo that is so attractive to Juliet, and what is it about Juliet that is so attractive to Romeo? In other words, what attracts each of them to the other?

Clearly Romeo is immediately struck by Juliet's beauty, but her beauty seems to make her vulnerable: it is a 'Beauty too rich for use, for earth too dear'. (Act 1 Scene 5). When Juliet talks about Romeo in Act 2 Scene 2 she too refers to Romeo's 'dear perfection'.

2   What external factors increase each character's attraction to the other?

Perhaps Juliet is desperate to escape marriage to Paris – a man she has no feelings for. She might also be desperate to escape a very restricting home life. Meanwhile Romeo might want to escape the suffocating attentions of his own parents and his friends.

Friar Lawrence

In two scenes the Friar thinks about the duality of things – how good things can also contain evil or be put to evil uses. Friar Lawrence is a wise and caring man who preaches peace, patience and self-restraint. He is shocked by Romeo's fickle feelings but agrees to marry Romeo and Juliet for an ulterior motive: to end the conflict between their two families.

The Nurse

The Nurse is an amusing character. Although she is a servant, she has a position of respect and some authority in the household, probably due to her role as joint mother and wet nurse to Juliet. Her self-importance makes her put on a show of refinement and dignity which is mocked by Mercutio. She torments Juliet by withholding the knowledge she has about the wedding arrangements. The Nurse likes to be the centre of attention.

Mercutio

This scene confirms what we already know about Mercutio: he loves word 'duelling'; he is full of wit – much of it of a bawdy type. He has no time for soppy, romantic love.

Love and doting

Friar Lawrence has already told Romeo off for 'doting' on Rosaline – being infatuated with her, but Romeo and Juliet are completely overwhelmed by their feelings for each other. Their love was at first sight, and so perhaps it is not surprising that they praise each other for what they *see*. Love is like a spell that is cast over people. The play often reminds us of the Cupid explanation for love: Cupid fires arrows blindly; whoever is struck falls in love immediately. The suggestion is that love is random and unexplainable.

Opposites and conflict

Conflict and contradiction underly everything in the play. Here Mercutio constantly engages others in verbal duels or battles of wit. Friar Lawrence notes how the medicinal herbs he gathers can both kill and cure. Death and life are intertwined: 'The earth that's nature's mother is her tomb' (Act 2 Scene 3). Even Romeo and Juliet's expressions of love in Act 2 Scene 2 are a sort of conflict – each of them trying to outdo the other in their expressions of love. Act 2 reinforces this sense of coexistence between opposites: conflict and peace; death and life; love and hate.

DEFINE IT!

bawdy humour – humour that is full of sexual references and suggestions

infatuated – loving obsessively rather than sensibly; if you are infatuated with someone, you won't see them for what they really are

innuendo – an implied meaning, usually a sexual one

wet nurse – an ordinary woman called in by wealthy families to breastfeed their children; wealthy families considered it undignified for their women to breastfeed

REVIEW IT!

1 How does Benvolio know where Romeo has gone?

2 According to Mercutio, who is the son of Venus?

3 Where is Juliet when Romeo sees her from the orchard?

4 When Romeo first hears Juliet speak, what is she wishing?

5 According to Romeo, how did he get into the orchard?

6 Why would a 'maiden blush bepaint' Juliet's cheek (Scene 2)?

7 Why is Juliet afraid that their love is 'too like the lightning' (Scene 2)?

8 What does Romeo fear is 'Too flattering sweet to be substantial'?

9 Why does Romeo want to be Juliet's 'bird'?

10 What is Friar Lawrence thinking about just before Romeo arrives?

11 What favour does Romeo ask of Friar Lawrence?

12 What shocks Friar Lawrence about Romeo's request?

13 Why does Friar Lawrence decide to give in to Romeo's request?

14 Give two examples of Mercutio's sarcasm.

15 Give an example of sexual innuendo that Mercutio uses to mock the Nurse.

16 What will Romeo's servant deliver to the Nurse, and why?

17 What methods does Juliet use to win the Nurse over?

18 Why is Juliet infuriated when the Nurse explains her inability to pass on her news by saying she is 'out of breath' (Scene 5)?

19 Imagine that Mercutio was arrested, and Romeo had to write a character reference for him. Write Romeo's summary of Mercutio's character based on what we learn about him in Act 2.

20 In Scene 3 Friar Lawrence is shocked by Romeo's sudden love for Juliet. He used to tell Romeo off not for loving girls, but for 'doting' on them – being infatuated. To what extent could Romeo and Juliet's love for each other be called 'doting'? Explain your views.

Act 3

Act 3 Scene 1

Summary: 'O, I am fortune's fool!'

Mercutio refuses to leave the street and accuses Benvolio of hypocrisy: he claims that Benvolio is the most quarrelsome man he knows, and always on the lookout for a fight. (As usual, Mercutio acts provocatively, his 'mad blood stirring' in the heat.)

As Benvolio feared, Capulets appear. Mercutio taunts Tybalt but Tybalt remains calm. When Romeo arrives, Tybalt calls him a villain and orders him to draw his sword. Romeo politely refuses, telling Tybalt that he now loves Capulets as much as he loves Montagues.

Mercutio is outraged by Romeo's 'submission' and draws his sword on Tybalt, who accepts the challenge. (Assumptions about manliness (and womanliness) are shown again here.) When Romeo tries to stop them, Tybalt stabs Mercutio under Romeo's arm. (Ironically, if Romeo had not tried to keep them apart, probably no one would have been hurt.)

Mercutio realises that he is dying. He curses the Montagues and Capulets and is helped away. Romeo feels that Juliet has softened him and taken away his manly courage. In anger he fights Tybalt and kills him.

At Benvolio's urging, Romeo runs away. When the Prince hears Benvolio's report of what happened, he is angry that his own 'kinsman', Mercutio, has been killed. He announces he will heavily fine the heads of both families. He banishes Romeo, warning that he will be executed if he is found in Verona.

Romeo

Romeo tries to prevent more senseless street fighting, showing that he values love over hate but the death of Mercutio reveals a different side to Romeo: he reacts angrily, thoughtlessly and on impulse. By accusing Juliet of making him 'effeminate' (unmanly) he regrets trying to be a calm peacemaker. Romeo is unpredictable and inconsistent.

DO IT!

Think carefully about how other modern readers/viewers might react to Romeo's words and behaviour in this scene.

STRETCH IT!

How do you think Shakespeare would have wanted his own audiences to react to Romeo?

There are a number of speeches in this scene that deserve close examination.

Extract 1

> **MERCUTIO**
>
> Men's eyes were made to look, and let them gaze.
> I will not budge for no man's pleasure, I.

Does this tell us that Mercutio likes to be the centre of attention at any cost? He is certainly very obstinate and will stand up to anyone – no matter the consequences. Does that make him brave or foolish?

Extract 2

Notice from this exchange of words Mercutio seems not to expect the fight to lead to serious injury: he only means to defeat Tybalt today (by taking away one of his nine lives) and 'dry-beat' rather than actually stab. Rapiers could be used as whips to inflict pain on your opponent without injuring them permanently.

> **TYBALT**
>
> What wouldst thou have with me?
>
> **MERCUTIO**
>
> Good King of Cats, nothing but one of your nine lives; that I mean to make bold withal, and, as you shall use me hereafter, dry-beat the rest of the eight.

Extracts 3 and 4

> **ROMEO**
>
> This day's black fate on moe days doth depend;
> This but begins the woe others must end.
>
> ---
>
> **ROMEO**
>
> O, I am fortune's fool.

Romeo gets the sense that this is the pivotal moment in his short life. From this point, tragedy becomes unavoidable. The sorrows that arise from his killing of Tybalt will only end by his death.

DO IT!

1 Write a *short* list of words that accurately describe Mercutio on the basis of his words here and of what you know of him from earlier in the play.

2 What other evidence earlier in the play might suggest that Mercutio did not want to kill or be killed by Tybalt? You could look at the beginning of Act 2 Scene 4.

DO IT!

Certainly Romeo is unlucky, but how far do you agree that he is a victim of fate? Could he have controlled events? Explain your views.

NAIL IT!

In your AQA exam you will be given an extract from the play as a starting point for your answer. Write about the extract carefully, but usually you will get more out of the extract if you think about it in the **context** of the whole play, or at least, when you compare the extract with other parts of the play. Don't hesitate to mention other relevant parts of the play when you write about the extract.

DEFINE IT!

effeminate – unmanly (often used as an insult)

kinsman – a blood relation

rapier – a long, thin sword with a pointed end but without sharpened edges; rapiers are normally used for sporting contests that are often called 'duels'

Act 3 Scene 2

Summary: Juliet hears of Romeo's banishment

Juliet is impatiently waiting for the night when she will lose her 'maidenhood' – her virginity – and be one with Romeo. (Juliet refers to Romeo as 'thou day in night'. Characters in the play often associate day and light with beauty and truth.) When Nurse arrives wailing 'he's dead', Juliet assumes she is talking about Romeo. Nurse provides gruesome details of the corpse 'all bedaub'd in blood'.

Finally, discovering that Romeo has killed Tybalt, Juliet is astonished that a creature as beautiful as Romeo could be guilty of such a crime. (Her descriptions are full of oxymorons including 'Beautiful tyrant, fiend angelical! Dove-feather'd raven, wolvish-ravening lamb!') The Nurse says you can't trust any man, and she wishes shame on Romeo.

This prompts Juliet to defend Romeo: 'Shall I speak ill of him that is my husband?' She points out that Tybalt was trying to kill her husband, and so she should be comforted that Romeo is alive more than upset that Tybalt is dead. Then she realises that Romeo has been banished, and she says that words cannot express the depth of her sorrow.

DEFINE IT!

bedaub'd – covered as though deliberately; often used for paint

She laments that the rope ladder will no longer be needed, and she will 'die maiden-widowed'. The Nurse now reveals that Romeo is hiding at Friar Lawrence's cell. She will tell him to come and comfort Juliet. Juliet gives the Nurse a ring to take to Romeo.

Light and dark

Light and dark are used as dramatic contrasts in the play. Night is something that hides secrets: it conceals the truth. Of course, that can be useful: Romeo and Juliet need to keep their feelings and their relationship secret, and Juliet sees dark and light interacting to the advantage of her and Romeo.

Light and dark are often presented as opposites that help, rather than negate, each other. Friar Lawrence has already pointed out that opposites coexist – even in people. Juliet is amazed at the paradox that 'such sweet flesh' as Romeo's could be a disguise for 'the spirit of a fiend' – a killer. The conclusion the Nurse draws from Juliet's thoughts is uncomplicated: all men are 'dissemblers': they deliberately conceal their true selves for their own advantage.

Why do you think the Nurse is still willing to help Romeo and Juliet if she has just been condemning Romeo as a killer?

DOIT!

Juliet asks, 'What storm is this that blows so contrary?'

- Make notes on some examples of opposites and contrasts in this scene.

- What is the significance of those opposites and contrasts? How do they add to the scene's impact?

Juliet's loyalty to Romeo

Extract 1

NURSE

Shame come to Romeo!

JULIET

Blister'd be thy tongue
For such a wish! He was not born to shame.
Upon his brow shame is asham'd to sit;
5 For 'tis a throne where honour may be crown'd
Sole monarch of the universal earth.
O what a beast was I to chide at him!

NURSE

Will you speak well of him that kill'd your cousin?

JULIET

Shall I speak ill of him that is my husband?
10 Ah, poor my lord, what tongue shall smooth thy name,
When I thy three-hours wife have mangl'd it?
But wherefore, villain, didst thou kill my cousin?
That villain cousin would have kill'd my husband.
Back, foolish tears, back to your native spring,
15 Your tributary drops belong to woe,
Which you mistaking offer up to joy.

These words create a violent and vivid image as Juliet turns the Nurse's shame-curse back on her.

The Nurse is a strong personality who does not hesitate to interrupt her social 'superiors', but even though she is only 13, Juliet stands up to her. She not only defends Romeo, she even praises him, using metaphors that present him as a king, someone who is above shame – even though he has killed a man.

These lines have a beautiful, elegant **rhythm** that makes Juliet sound full of confidence and authority. It is as though she is making a powerful speech in public. She is very mature for her age!

Tears are meant to express sadness, but Juliet has made them express her joy instead. After Juliet's doubts in the previous lines, she is now assertive and sure. She is controlling her body, and by extension, controlling nature.

Find some other parts of the play where Juliet shows her strength. Think of some words that might help to sum up her strength in those scenes. Complete the table below to record your findings.

Scene	Details	Strength words
Act 1 Scene 3	Juliet remains politely non-committal to her mother's recommendation of Paris as a husband.	Firm (with the Nurse), diplomatic, respectful, crafty
Act 2 Scene 5		

AQA exam-style question

Starting with the conversation in extract 1 above, explore how far Shakespeare presents Juliet as a strong female character in *Romeo and Juliet*.

Write about:

- how Shakespeare presents Juliet in this conversation
- how far Shakespeare presents Juliet as a strong female character in the play as a whole.

[30 marks]

Act 3 Scene 3

Summary: 'Hold thy desperate hand'

Romeo is hiding in Friar Lawrence's cell. Friar Lawrence fears that Romeo is enjoying his latest 'calamity', and tells Romeo he should be grateful to the Prince for banishing rather than executing him. Romeo insists that banishment is the same as death.

Romeo angrily rejects Friar Lawrence's advice to be patient and not waste time complaining about circumstances that can't be changed. Friar Lawrence says only madmen won't listen to advice, but Romeo implies that Friar Lawrence is being unwise by ignoring his distress. He claims that Friar Lawrence is not acknowledging Romeo's problems because he is not young and in love, and so he can't understand Romeo's feeling that he might as well be dead.

The Nurse arrives and orders Romeo to 'be a man'. She reports that Juliet does nothing but weep, fall down and call out 'Tybalt' and then 'Romeo'. Romeo concludes that his name is killing Juliet, and he tries to stab himself. The Nurse disarms him.

Romeo's sinful attempted suicide enrages Friar Lawrence. He tells Romeo he should be ashamed of behaving like a beast or a woman. The Friar tells Romeo to be grateful for his 'pack of blessings': he is good-looking and intelligent, he is in love, Juliet is still alive, Tybalt – his would-be killer – is dead, and he has been banished rather than executed.

Friar Lawrence tells Romeo to go to Mantua until the Friar can publicise his marriage to Juliet, and persuade the Prince to pardon him. The Nurse is impressed with this advice because it clearly shows 'learning'.

Romeo is comforted to receive Juliet's ring from the Nurse. Friar Lawrence warns Romeo to leave Juliet before dawn so that he can safely escape from Verona.

Friar Lawrence's view of Romeo

Friar Lawrence is often exasperated by Romeo's behaviour. He feels Romeo is too self-absorbed. He accuses Romeo of being 'wedded to calamity', as though he is in love with it.

Friar Lawrence and the Nurse believe Romeo should 'man up' in the face of misfortune. The Friar suspects that Romeo actually enjoys misfortune. This is behind his comment to the Nurse that Romeo is 'with his own tears made drunk'.

 STRETCH IT!

The Nurse's sudden arrival prevents Friar Lawrence from replying to Romeo's speech that starts with 'Thou canst not speak…' and ends with '…an unmade grave.' What do you think the Friar would have said if he and Romeo had not been interrupted? Write the Friar's reply.

'Art thou a man?'

Characters in *Romeo and Juliet* often behave in ways that fit assumptions about the different sexes – male and female. Juliet is protected almost to the point of imprisonment not just because she is young, but also because she is female. All characters value 'manliness' in men, and this view of 'manliness' guides characters' expectations of men. *Romeo and Juliet* was written hundreds of years ago, but it is still performed today. How *you* react to this idea of manliness is a valid aspect of the play's *context* because the meaning of this old play will partly depend on the reactions of a modern audience.

DO IT!

Think about your answers to these two questions:

- Is Romeo unmanly?
- Does it matter how manly he is?

Extract 1

> **NURSE**
> O, he is even in my mistress' case.
> Just in her case! O woeful sympathy!
> Piteous predicament! Even so lies she,
> Blubbering and weeping, weeping and blubbering.
> 5 Stand up, stand up; stand, and you be a man:
> For Juliet's sake, for her sake, rise and stand;
> Why should you fall into so deep an O?

The Nurse observes that both Romeo and Juliet – despite their different sexes – are in the same state of distress.

What tone of voice might the Nurse use for the this line? Sympathy? Disgust?

The Nurse is hard on Romeo. She believes he should be 'manly' for Juliet's sake.

Extract 2

Here is that idea of 'seeming' again: *seeming* to be one thing (here a man) but underneath *being* something else (here a woman or a beast).

> **FRIAR LAWRENCE**
> Hold thy desperate hand:
> Art thou a man? Thy form cries out thou art.
> Thy tears are womanish, thy wild acts denote
> The unreasonable fury of a beast.
> 5 Unseemly woman in a seeming man!
> And ill-beseeming beast in seeming both!

It is not enough to *be* a man, according to Friar Lawrence; a man needs to behave in a manly way. Presumably, Romeo should suppress his feelings and not cry.

Extract 3

> **FRIAR LAWRENCE**
> Thy noble shape is but a form of wax,
> Digressing from the valour of a man;

When the Nurse called Paris 'a man of wax' (Act 1 Scene 3), she meant he was perfect, but the Friar is criticising Romeo for being mere wax – a man only in appearance. The 'manly' virtue that Romeo lacks is bravery.

NAIL IT!

- In your AQA exam it is OK to explore your personal response, but do explain your views with reference to details in the text.

- To indicate that you are exploring *possible* interpretations, use tentative words such as 'perhaps', 'this could'/'might', 'suggest'/'imply'.

DEFINE IT!

denote – show

digressing – moving away

piteous – pitiful

predicament – condition, tricky situation

valour – bravery

Act 3 Scene 4

Summary: 'She will be rul'd'

Capulet offers Juliet to Paris as his wife, and sets Thursday – three days later – for the wedding. He decides on a small wedding out of respect for the death of Tybalt.

Note how Juliet no longer has choice; she is now expected just to obey.

Act 3 Scene 5

Summary: Arrangements for Juliet's marriage to Paris are made

In contrast to the violence of the double killing and the resulting misery and despair, this scene is calm, poetic and romantic.

In bed with Juliet, Romeo says that because it is getting light he must 'be gone and live, or stay and die'. When Juliet insists that it is not yet morning, Romeo says he is willing to stay even at risk of arrest and execution.

Suddenly, Juliet realises that it is morning and urges Romeo to 'be gone'. As Romeo climbs down the rope ladder, Juliet gets an image of him in his grave. (Note the foreshadowing Shakespeare uses here to remind us that the plot is heading towards tragedy.) He reassures her before leaving for Mantua.

Juliet's mother comes in and assumes Juliet is crying because Romeo – Tybalt's murderer – still lives. Throughout their conversation, Juliet replies ambiguously.

However, when Lady Capulet announces the 'good news' that Juliet's father has arranged her immediate marriage to Paris, Juliet fiercely rejects the plan. She craftily claims she'd rather marry 'Romeo, whom you know I hate' than Paris.

Capulet is infuriated to hear of Juliet's disobedience and threatens to drag her to the wedding. He hurls abuse at Juliet, calling her a 'curse' on them. When the Nurse tries to calm him, Capulet turns his abuse on her.

Capulet threatens to throw Juliet out to 'die in the streets'. Juliet appeals to her mother, but she says 'I have done with thee'. (This is an intense and shocking event. Even Lady Capulet and the Nurse are horrified at Lord Capulet's sudden violent abuse directed at his own daughter.)

Juliet pretends to accept the Nurse's astonishing advice to marry Paris because he is better than Romeo, and Romeo is as good as dead. She asks the Nurse to tell her parents that she will confess to Friar Lawrence her sin of disobedience.

When the Nurse leaves, Juliet condemns her as a 'wicked fiend' and decides to visit Friar Lawrence. If he has no solution, she will kill herself.

Write a paragraph explaining why Lord Capulet speaks and behaves how he does.

What do you think of the Nurse's advice? Is she just being realistic? Is she a traitor to Juliet?

Extract 1

> **CAPULET**
>
> Out, you green-sickness carrion! Out, you baggage!
> You tallow-face!
>
> **LADY CAPULET**
>
> Fie, fie! What, are you mad?
>
> **JULIET**
>
> Good father, I beseech you on my knees,
> 5 Hear me with patience but to speak a word.
>
> **CAPULET**
>
> Hang thee, young baggage! disobedient wretch!
> I tell thee what, – get thee to church a' Thursday,
> Or never after look me in the face.
> Speak not, reply not, do not answer me!
> 10 My fingers itch. Wife, we scarce thought us blest
> That God had lent us but this only child;
> But now I see this one is one too much,
> And that we have a curse in having her.
> Out on her, hilding!
>
> **NURSE**
>
> 15 God in heaven bless her!
> You are to blame, my lord, to rate her so.
>
> **CAPULET**
>
> And why, my lady wisdom? Hold your tongue,
> Good prudence; smatter with your gossips, go.

These are highly visual, disgusting insults that are shocking in their venom and violence.

Juliet's words suggest that she is trying to appease her father by treating him like a priest, a holy man. This enhances the sense of her innocence and purity.

Capulet's anger is emphasised by his string of harsh imperative verbs and verb phrases.

Capulet's verbal violence is in danger of tipping into physical violence.

Capulet wishes they had never had Juliet, even though she is their only child. She is a 'curse' to them and worthless ('hilding').

Here the Nurse protects herself with God's authority and by addressing Capulet respectfully as 'my lord'.

Capulet's response is sarcastic and contemptuous.

DEFINE IT!

carrion – dead animals eaten by other animals

hilding – something that is worthless

tallow-face – candles were made of tallow (animal fat), so Juliet's face is pale and waxy

AQA exam-style question

Shakespeare presents Lord Capulet as a power-mad bully in *Romeo and Juliet*.

Starting with the conversation in extract 1 above, explore how far you agree with this opinion.

Write about:

- how far Shakespeare presents Lord Capulet as a power-mad bully in this conversation
- how far Shakespeare presents Lord Capulet as a power-mad bully in the play as a whole.

[30 marks]

 **STRETCH IT!**

Compare Lord Capulet in this scene with what we know about him from earlier scenes.

Character and theme essentials

Romeo

Romeo is unlucky in Act 3. He tries to stop the fight between Mercutio and Tybalt. His guilt, grief and anger prompt him to kill Tybalt. Friar Lawrence has a different view of Romeo's character: he accuses Romeo of being self-indulgent, dramatic and unmanly. In bed with Juliet we see another Romeo: romantic, loving, protective.

Juliet

Juliet shows her strength and maturity in defying her parents and fighting for her independence.

Mercutio

Even as he is dying, Mercutio continues to be a joker: 'Ask for me tomorrow, and you shall find me a grave man.' (Act 3 Scene 1). Perhaps Mercutio only meant to fight Tybalt for sport. He waves his sword at Tybalt, taunting him with 'here's that shall make you dance'. (Act 3 Scene 1).

Friar Lawrence

Romeo and Juliet both seek Friar Lawrence's judgement and advice, but his plan to get Romeo's banishment overturned – and to publicise the lovers' secret marriage – is very ambitious.

Lord Capulet

We see Lord Capulet's violent and dictatorial side. Earlier he told Paris he would allow Juliet to marry whoever she pleased, but now he 'gives' her to Paris as though he owns her.

The Nurse

In advising Juliet to forget her marriage to Romeo, the Nurse is just being realistic, but this advice changes her from trusted adviser to 'wicked fiend!' (Act 3 Scene 5) in Juliet's eyes.

Fate

When Romeo hears of Mercutio's death, he senses 'This day's black fate' (Act 3 Scene 1). When he kills Tybalt, he sees himself as a helpless victim: 'O, I am fortune's fool' (Act 3 Scene 1). Juliet too is haunted by this sense of unavoidable, tragic fate when she has a vision of Romeo 'As one dead in the bottom of a tomb' (Act 3 Scene 5). Romeo and Juliet certainly see themselves as helpless victims of fate, but their own actions and attitudes contribute to their fate.

Opposites

The battle between Montagues and Capulets ends in death at the beginning of Act 3, and this ongoing feud is the backdrop to all the conflict in the play. However, as Friar Lawrence points out in Act 2 Scene 3, conflict and contradiction also play out in individual people. Juliet is astonished that 'a gorgeous palace' (Act 3 Scene 2) like Romeo could contain the ability to murder. His beautiful outside must be deceitful, untrustworthy:

'O serpent heart, hid with a flow'ring face!' (Act 3 Scene 2) The idea of opposites is also expressed in the repeated references to night and day, light and dark. However, darkness and night are not symbols of evil. Darkness helps the two secret lovers; daylight is the threat. Juliet pleads, 'Come gentle night,' (Act 3 Scene 2) as she waits for Romeo's arrival.

Masculinity

Macho banter and posturing fuels the tragedy of Scene 1: 'I will not budge for no man's pleasure, I' Mercutio asserts proudly and provocatively. Tybalt's killing of Mercutio makes Romeo ashamed that his love for Juliet has made him 'effeminate' and taken away his manly bravery. Later Friar Lawrence condemns Romeo's tears of despair as 'womanish' (Act 3 Scene 3). He shames Romeo by asking him 'Art thou a man?' Modern readers might be less impressed by these ideas about manliness, but it is worth asking yourself how Shakespeare might have expected the audience to feel about manliness.

REVIEW IT!

1 Of what does Mercutio accuse Benvolio?

2 Romeo tells Tybalt that he loves him. Why does Romeo love him?

3 In what way does Romeo consider Juliet to be a cause of Mercutio's death?

4 How do we know that the Prince is related to Mercutio?

5 In her speech at the beginning of Scene 2, why does Juliet praise the night?

6 When Juliet expresses astonishment that someone as beautiful as Romeo could have done something so ugly as killing another man, what is the Nurse's response?

7 What does Juliet send to Romeo to show her continued loyalty to him?

8 Why does Romeo not agree with Friar Lawrence that the Prince has been kind in banishing Romeo rather than executing him?

9 What reason does Romeo give for believing that Friar Lawrence can't understand his feelings?

10 Who stops Romeo from killing himself?

11 What does Friar Lawrence mean when he tells Romeo, 'Thy noble shape is but a form of wax.' (Scene 3)?

12 What is Friar Lawrence's plan to solve the disaster that has befallen Romeo and Juliet?

13 Why does Capulet decide to have *only* a small wedding for Juliet?

14 Juliet claims that she and Romeo are not hearing the song of the lark but of another bird. Which bird?

15 Why does Lord Capulet accuse Juliet of ingratitude (Scene 5)?

16 What advice does The Nurse give Juliet (Scene 5)?

17 What might Romeo mean when he says that the 'black fate' of this day 'begins the woe others must end' (Scene 1)?

18 As Romeo leaves Juliet's bedroom, Juliet says 'Oh God! I have an ill-divining soul!'. What does she mean (Scene 5)?

19 Why does Lady Capulet ask her husband if he is mad (Scene 5)?

20 How could Act 3 be considered the 'tipping point' or 'fulcrum' of the whole play?

Act 4

DO IT!

- Make a list of the ways in which Juliet shows her bravery and determination in this scene.

- Think about how *you* would think and feel if you were in Juliet's position.

DEFINE IT!

chapless – jawless

charnel-house – a building containing bones and/or bodies of less 'important' citizens

reeky – stinking

shanks – legs

Act 4 Scene 1

Summary: Friar Lawrence's desperate plan for Juliet

Friar Lawrence tells Paris he is unhappy with the haste of his marriage with Juliet – especially as it is not clear what Juliet wants. Paris explains that Capulet has brought the wedding forward to distract Juliet from her grief for Tybalt.

When Juliet arrives, she cleverly avoids telling Paris she loves him. When Paris leaves, Juliet tells Friar Lawrence she is desperate enough to kill herself if the Friar cannot save her from marrying Paris.

Friar Lawrence tells Juliet that he has a 'desperate' plan that depends on her bravery. Juliet replies that she would rather do anything, however terrifying, to avoid the shame of being unfaithful to Romeo.

The Friar gives Juliet a potion to make her look dead for 42 hours. While she is buried in the family vault, Friar Lawrence will write to Romeo telling him about the plan. Romeo and the Friar will release Juliet from the tomb, and Romeo will take her to Mantua. The Friar tells Juliet the plan will work as long as she is determined and not put off by 'womanish fear'. Juliet agrees to the plan.

Extract 1

"

JULIET
O, bid me leap, rather than marry Paris,
From off the battlements of any tower;
Or walk in thievish ways; or bid me lurk
Where serpents are; chain me with roaring bears,
5   Or hide me nightly in a charnel-house,
O'ercover'd quite with dead men's rattling bones,
With reeky shanks and yellow chapless skulls;
Or bid me go into a new-made grave,
And hide me with a dead man in his shroud -
10 Things that to hear them told have made me tremble -
And I will do it without fear or doubt,
To live an unstain'd wife to my sweet love.

"

Juliet vividly describes a number of ghastly, terrifying situations that she would consider preferable to marriage with Paris.

These **noun phrases** make the dangers very physical and direct. The long 'e' sound in 'reeks' and the 'sh' and 's' sounds in 'shanks' stretch the sound of the phrase, making it sound even more revolting.

The lines in this speech are in iambic pentameter (some with slight variation), the last two lines being very neat iambic pentameter. The tidy rhythm of these lines make Juliet's words neater and more decisive.

Iambic pentameter

Iambs give a line a dee-dum, dee-dum regular rhythm. However, if all lines were spoken with an inflexible 'dee-dum' rhythm then their subtlety and meaning would become lost, and the effect would be very tiresome for the audience. Actors must decide which syllables should be stressed for meaning.

STRETCHIT!

Look at Act 3 Scene 1 from Benvolio: 'Be my head…' down to Tybalt: 'turn and draw'. Notice where the script switches from prose to verse (or the other way round). Read aloud the lines either side of the switch. Ask yourself these questions:

- Why do you think Shakespeare switched between forms here?

- How does the tone of the scene change after the switch?

NAILIT!

In your AQA exam it is better to think of iambic pentameter as the underlying form of Shakespeare's poetry, rather than being a mathematical rule.

AQA exam-style question

Starting with the speech in extract 1 above, explore how Shakespeare presents Juliet as a brave woman in *Romeo and Juliet*.

Write about:

- how Shakespeare presents Juliet in this speech

- how Shakespeare presents Juliet as a brave woman in the play as a whole.

[30 marks]

Act 4 Scene 2

Summary: 'I'll have this knot knit up tomorrow morning'

Capulet is pleased to hear that Juliet has gone to Friar Lawrence. When Juliet returns she asks her father's forgiveness, and promises to obey him in future. Delighted, Capulet decides to bring forward the wedding to the following morning. He says the whole city should be grateful to Friar Lawrence for reclaiming Juliet from sin and foolishness. (Obedience is very important to Lord Capulet. Notice how he gives orders to his wife and makes decisions about the wedding without consulting her.)

Power and authority

In *Romeo and Juliet*, Verona is a hierarchical society: beneath the Prince are the heads of the most powerful families. Lord Capulet rules his family, expecting his wife and daughter to obey. Others have to carry out Capulet's orders – even when they are unreasonable. Friar Lawrence's authority is not based on power but on the respect he earns by being wise and holy ('reverend').

Act 4 Scene 3

Summary: Juliet's terrors

Juliet sends away her mother and the Nurse. Now she is overcome with mounting fears: perhaps the potion will not work, or perhaps it will kill her, or she might wake in the tomb only to suffocate, or be driven mad by the horrible sights, smells and sounds around her. Finally, she calms herself and drinks Friar Lawrence's potion. (Again Juliet shows her bravery and self-control: it is not that she has no fears but that she conquers her fears that is so impressive.)

Ask yourself how *you* would feel about carrying out the Friar's plan if you were in Juliet's position.

Act 4 Scene 4

Compare Capulet here with the impression we get of him in the feast scene – Act 1 Scene 5.

Summary: Final preparations for the wedding

In the early hours of the morning the Capulet household is busily preparing for the wedding. The Nurse and Lady Capulet try to make Capulet stop interfering and go to bed. Suddenly, they hear Paris arriving with his musicians, so Capulet sends the Nurse to get Juliet ready. (Notice how the bumbling, interfering side of Capulet is again on show here.)

 STRETCHIT!

Many performances of *Romeo and Juliet* leave out this short comic scene.

- Why do you think it might sometimes be left out?
- What might be gained or lost by leaving it out?

Act 4 Scene 5

Look at the characters' attitudes towards death. Notice how Juliet's 'death' brings out different feelings towards her.

Summary: 'She's dead, deceas'd, she's dead, alack the day!'

The Nurse finds Juliet deeply asleep. When she tries to wake her, she believes that Juliet is dead. Lady Capulet comes in and joins in with the Nurse's wailing. Capulet arrives but finds that death 'Ties up my tongue and will not let me speak.' Paris arrives and is also devastated by what 'Most detestable death' has done. Capulet's earlier anger and revulsion towards Juliet are now forgotten: 'with my child my joys are buried.'

Friar Lawrence, who arrives with Paris, tells them they should be ashamed. They wanted the best for Juliet, and now she has got it: 'eternal life' in heaven. He tells them to dry their tears and prepare Juliet for burial. Capulet says that all the things they had gathered for the wedding they will now use for the funeral: 'all things change them to the contrary'. (Friar Lawrence makes quite sure that the characters learn important lessons from Juliet's 'death'. He knows that to learn they must suffer.)

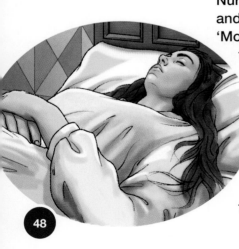

They exit, leaving the musicians and servants. One servant, Peter, gets into an argument with the musicians. They insult each other until Peter draws his dagger. He calms down but again insults the musicians before leaving. Outraged, they decide to get what they can now their wedding job has been cancelled. They decide to 'stay [*for*] dinner.'

Extract 1

CAPULET
O son, the night before thy wedding day
Hath death lain with thy bride. There she lies,
Flower as she was, deflowered by him.

Death is presented as a living and malicious creature that has had sex with Juliet, taking away her virginity. The underlined words extend this image of death as a sort of demon bridegroom. For a modern audience, this could be a shocking image.

Extract 2

PARIS
Beguil'd, divorced, wronged, spited, slain!
Most detestable death, by thee beguil'd,
By cruel, cruel thee quite overthrown!

Again, Paris treats death not as something that happens by chance, but as the deliberate aim of a hated, cruel and cunning creature. The final word, 'overthrown', emphasises that death has won an ongoing battle with Juliet. We know that Juliet's siblings have already lost that battle.

Extract 3

FRIAR LAWRENCE
Dry up your tears, and stick your rosemary
On this fair corse, and, as the custom is,
And in her best array, bear her to church;
For though fond nature bids us all lament,
Yet nature's tears are reason's merriment.

The Friar's advice is surprisingly direct and harsh in the circumstances.

In these final two lines Friar Lawrence says it's natural but unreasonable to cry. Our powers of reason should make us rejoice that Juliet is now in a wonderful place – heaven. Note how the last two lines suddenly rhyme to give the advice neatness and authority.

Extract 4

FRIAR LAWRENCE
The heavens do lower upon you for some ill;
Move them no more by crossing their high will.

Again, the Friar's rhyme could make the advice sound neat and casual, and his comment that heaven 'do lower upon you' suggests that they themselves have caused Juliet's death through some 'ill' – some sin they have done.

DO IT!

Write a paragraph in answer to these two questions:

1 What 'ill' have the Capulets done that might have displeased heaven?

2 What is Friar Lawrence trying to achieve in this scene?

DEFINE IT!

beguil'd – tricked, lied to

corse – corpse, dead body

deflower – to end a woman's virginity

Character and theme essentials

Juliet

Although Juliet becomes frenzied when she becomes overcome with 'hideous fears' of waking up in the family tomb; overall she is self-controlled, determined, practical and very brave. She is also perceptive enough to realise that Friar Lawrence might be tricking her into actually killing herself in order to get her out of the way and save himself from being 'dishonour'd' by her 'illegal' marriage to Romeo. Perhaps she believes that as a female she is less important than the honour of a priest. Even today there are many cases of priests' reputations being protected by cover ups.

Friar Lawrence

Friar Lawrence shows great compassion for Juliet and her situation. His plan to save her draws on his expert knowledge of herbs, but it also depends on his daring and his cunning. It is complex, risky and, as he says, 'desperate' (Act 4 Scene 1). Juliet worries whether she can trust him: does he have ulterior motives? One of his ulterior motives would explain the harsh way he treats the Capulets in their grief over Juliet's 'death': he wants them to learn from this experience and to become better, humbler, more tolerant people.

How we feel about Friar Lawrence is significant. In Shakespeare's time priests were viewed with respect as servants of God, but also sometimes with suspicion for being greedy and crafty rather than purely holy.

Power and authority

One dimension of power demonstrated in the play is men's control of women. We saw in earlier scenes how Lord Capulet considers Juliet to be his property to be given away to another man – Paris – if he sees fit. In Act 4, it is clear that in marriage Juliet will be owned by Paris: 'Thy face is mine,' he informs her gently (Act 4 Scene 1). The only way Juliet can get temporary freedom from this enforced husband is by claiming the protection of another man – her priest.

Verona is not a democracy in the play, it is a hierarchy – a pyramid of power. Lord Capulet is near the top (although he has to obey the Prince). Capulet expects – and mainly gets – obedience from his family and followers, and he becomes violent if his authority is challenged. Juliet's only real power is whether to live or die, and in Act 4 she shows she is quite ready to kill herself as a means of escape.

Friar Lawrence is not a rich man, but he has some power and authority that comes from his position as a priest, and also from the respect that other powerful characters have for him. Of course, Friar Lawrence wants the Capulets (and presumably the Montagues too) to accept that ultimate power is with God ('the heavens'). The Friar hopes that if they recognise divine power, the family leaders will use their own power more humbly, kindly and responsibly.

Death

Death is **personified** and is presented as a cruel and devious enemy, perhaps reflecting how common unexpected death was at the time: most members of Shakespeare's audience would regularly have had to grieve the death of loved ones. What is disturbing to a modern audience is how death, sex and love are intertwined in *Romeo and Juliet*. This connection is particularly clear in Capulet's reaction to Juliet's death when he tells Paris, that death has 'lain with thy bride.' (Scene 5). Disturbing too is Juliet's vivid imaginings of the physical and supernatural aspects of death: the 'foul mouth' of the vault (Scene 3) where 'the bones…are pack'd' and there are 'loathsome smells'. She imagines herself playing 'with my forefathers' joints' and madly smashing out her own brains with 'some great kinsman's bone'.

REVIEW IT!

1 What does Paris (and Capulet) believe to be the cause of Juliet's 'immoderate' crying?

2 What sort of kiss does Paris give Juliet as he leaves her?

3 How does Juliet intend to kill herself if Friar Lawrence cannot suggest an effective solution to her problem?

4 For how long will Juliet sleep after she drinks Friar Lawrence's 'distilled liquor' (Scene 1)?

5 How will Peter guarantee to find only good cooks?

6 What excuse does Juliet give the Nurse to persuade her to leave Juliet alone in her bedroom?

7 Of what does Juliet briefly suspect Friar Lawrence?

8 How does the Nurse try to persuade Capulet to go to bed?

9 What time does Paris arrive to wake up Juliet?

10 What surprises the Nurse about Juliet when she draws the curtains?

11 By whom, according to Capulet, has Juliet been 'deflowered' (Scene 5)?

12 How does Peter insult the musicians?

13 What do the musicians decide to do?

14 Briefly explain how Juliet deals with Paris at the start of Act 4?

15 How does Capulet react when Juliet begs his pardon?

16 What effect on the audience might be created by Juliet's description of Tybalt as 'festering in his shroud' (Scene 3)?

17 What impression do we get of Capulet in Scene 4?

18 What view of death does Paris show in Scene 5?

19 Read Capulet's speech in Scene 5 ('All things that we ordained…to the contrary'). How does this speech extend the idea of opposites that runs through the play?

20 Explain why Friar Lawrence said to the Capulets (and Paris): 'The heavens do lower upon you for some ill/Move them no more by crossing their high will.'

Act 5

Act 5 Scene 1

Summary: Romeo buys poison

Romeo is feeling unusually cheerful because he has had a dream that he believes foretells 'some joyful news'. Although in his dream Juliet found him dead, she brought him back to life with a kiss. He marvels that if this dream – the sweet 'shadow' of love – is 'so rich in joy', then how much sweeter the real thing will be. (Dramatic irony: at this point – just as he is about to receive very bad news – Romeo is unusually optimistic.)

Balthasar arrives with the news that Juliet is dead: 'Her body sleeps in Capels' monument'. He asks for Romeo's forgiveness for having to bring such bad news. (More irony: sleep is a **euphemism** for death, but unknown to Balthasar, Juliet is literally asleep.)

Balthasar tells Romeo he has no letters from Friar Lawrence. Romeo sends Balthasar for 'ink and paper' and horses, and then reveals to us that he is going to poison himself next to Juliet's body. He visits an apothecary who he knows to be so poor that he will agree to sell Romeo deadly poison. He sets off for the Capulet tomb with the poison, which he calls a 'cordial' as it will cure him. (This reminds us of Friar Lawrence's earlier thoughts about the dual properties of 'medicines': they can both kill and cure (Act 2 Scene 3).)

Act 5 Scene 2

Summary: The undelivered letter

Friar John, who was meant to take the letter to Romeo, brings bad news to Friar Lawrence: Friar John was quarantined in a house as part of a plague precaution and so he could not deliver the letter. When Friar Lawrence hears the bad news he exclaims, 'Unhappy fortune!' (In other words, fate is against him. His plan has been ruined by bad luck.) Friar Lawrence immediately realises that this 'may do much danger'. He sends Friar John for a crowbar to break open the tomb. He decides to write again to Romeo, asking him to come to his cell, where he will keep Juliet until Romeo arrives.

Tragedy

Romeo and Juliet is known as a tragedy. A traditional tragedy is not merely something that turns out unhappily; it has certain ingredients: a high-ranking, respected person enjoys a great many advantages in life. He (or she) is happy. Their life then falls into disaster and sorrow through a combination of bad luck, fate and weaknesses in their own character. Despite their weaknesses, we tend to sympathise with the character, and that makes us feel the tragedy more powerfully. Roughly speaking, Romeo fits this model of a tragic hero.

DOIT!

Complete the table below to explore the extent to which Romeo fits the model of a tragic hero. Some detail has been suggested to start you off.

Ways in which Romeo is a tragic hero	Evidence to support
High-ranking, respected person	Heir to wealth and power: only son of powerful Lord Montague.
Enjoys advantages/is happy	
Fate	
Bad luck	
Character weaknesses	

Extract 1

Romeo's optimism is mixed with his typical distrust of fate: he wonders *if* he can trust what his dream showed, and he suspects 'truth' of 'flattering' – deceiving – him.

ROMEO

If I may trust the flattering truth of sleep,
My dreams presage some joyful news at hand.
My bosom's lord sits lightly in his throne,
And all this day an unaccustom'd spirit
5 Lifts me above the ground with cheerful thoughts.
I dreamt my lady came and found me dead, –
Strange dream, that gives a dead man leave to think! –
And breath'd such life with kisses in my lips,
That I reviv'd, and was an emperor.
10 Ah me, how sweet is love itself possess'd,
When but love's shadows are so rich in joy.

Despite his dream, Romeo is unusually light-hearted in this speech: his words (highlighted) are light and humorous. He even jokes to himself about a 'dead man' (sleeping man) being allowed to think. Of course, there is an ironic connection between death and sleep in the case of Juliet.

AQA exam-style question

'In *Romeo and Juliet* Shakespeare presents fate as cruel and spiteful.'

Starting with the speech in extract 1 above, explore how far you agree with this opinion.

Write about:

- how far Shakespeare presents fate as cruel and/or spiteful in this speech
- how far Shakespeare presents fate as cruel and/or spiteful in the play as a whole.

[30 marks]

DEFINE IT!

presage – predict; foretell

DO IT!

Find examples of fate being presented as cruel and/or spiteful in the play.

Romeo threatens Balthasar to make him go. Is there a violent, bullying streak in Romeo?

Act 5 Scene 3

Summary: Romeo and Juliet kill themselves

Before daylight, Paris arrives at Juliet's tomb. Romeo arrives, dismisses Balthasar and begins to force open the tomb.

When Paris tries to arrest Romeo, Romeo fights and kills him. Feeling sorry for Paris, Romeo lays his body in the tomb.

Romeo is amazed Juliet still looks beautiful and alive. He fears that death is keeping Juliet for a lover. (This is another example of a macabre personification of death, again as a sort of demon bridegroom. This association of death and sex is a disturbing one.) He vows to stay and protect her, so he drinks the poison and dies.

Friar Lawrence finds the bodies of Romeo and Paris. Juliet wakes and the Friar fails to get her to come away with him. Hearing the watch coming, the Friar leaves. Finding that Romeo has left her no poison, Juliet kills herself with his dagger. (The double death scene is famously poignant: Juliet realises from Romeo's warm lips that she woke just too late.)

Balthasar and Friar Lawrence are caught. The Prince, Montague and the Capulets arrive. Friar Lawrence explains everything that has happened. A letter that Romeo left for his father confirms the Friar's account.

In their grief, Montague and Capulet are reconciled. The Prince announces that 'Some shall be pardon'd, and some punished.' (Shakespeare uses the Prince to draw out the lessons of the play for us: 'See what a scourge is laid upon your hate,' he tells Montague and Capulet.)

Pardoned or punished?

The Prince says that 'All are punish'd' by the suffering ('woe') that they have caused themselves. However, his announcement that 'Some shall be pardon'd, and some punished' seems to suggest he has further punishment in mind for some of those involved. His use of the future tense 'shall' implies that he might hand out pardons and punishments after he has fully investigated the matter.

STRETCH IT!

To what extent might Shakespeare want us to see Romeo and/or Juliet as responsible for their own deaths?

Give reasons for your thoughts.

DO IT!

Who or what do you think is most to blame for what happened to Romeo and Juliet? Give reasons for your thoughts.

Extract 1

At the end of the play the Prince urges the family heads to learn the lessons from the results of their violent feud.

"

PRINCE

Where be these enemies? Capulet, Montague,
See what a scourge is laid upon your hate,
That heaven finds means to kill your joys with love!
And I for winking at your discords too
5 Have lost a brace of kinsmen: all are punish'd.

CAPULET

O brother Montague, give me thy hand.
This is my daughter's jointure, for no more
Can I demand.

MONTAGUE

But I can give thee more,
10 For I will raise her statue in pure gold,
That whiles Verona by that name is known,
There shall no figure at such rate be set
As that of true and faithful Juliet.

CAPULET

As rich shall Romeo's by his lady's lie,
15 Poor sacrifices of our enmity!

"

> The tone of the Prince's words is probably scornful: the two families' conflict is pointless and they have both lost from it. 'Scourge' has a harsh, violent sound, helping to emphasise the Prince's bitterness.
>
> Everyone has been punished through the results of their folly; their punishment is their grief.

> The result of the tragedy of Romeo and Juliet is the reconciliation of their two families.

> Notice the neatness of Montague's final two lines. The sudden rhymes give the lines added finality and authority, showing Montague's sincerity. You can imagine the lines inscribed on Juliet's statue.

> Capulet's use of rhyme mirrors Montague's, thus conveying their new unity. ('Enmity' and 'lie' were probably pronounced so as to rhyme.)

AQA exam-style question

Starting with extract 1 above, explore how Shakespeare presents justice in *Romeo and Juliet*.

Write about:

- how Shakespeare presents justice in this extract

- how Shakespeare presents justice in the play as a whole.

[30 marks]

First, study the question carefully and annotate it so that you fully understand it. (For more advice on understanding questions see pages 82–83.)

Make some brief notes for each paragraph of your answer.

- Refer to at least three other points in the play where justice is an important issue.

- Plan to comment on the effects of a few brief, relevant quotations

- Plan to refer to relevant, useful aspects of context.

DEFINE IT!

enmity – hatred

feud – a disagreement and conflict that goes on forever

jointure – dowry; the bride's father was expected to make a dowry payment to the bridegroom.

reconciliation – putting aside differences and coming to an agreement

scourge – punishment through suffering

Character and theme essentials

Romeo

Certainly there is something sad and heroically self-sacrificing about Romeo's suicide. The audience is made to suffer by knowing that his suicide is completely unnecessary: Juliet is about to wake up. There is another side to Romeo on show in the final act though: firstly, he exploits a poor apothecary, forcing him to provide poison against his better judgement. Secondly, he kills Paris. True, he warns him, and after he has killed him and discovered his identity he pities him by laying him in the tomb, 'a triumphant grave' (Act 5 Scene 3), but his attack on Paris is typically hot-tempered and enthusiastic: 'Then have at thee, boy!' (Act 5 Scene 3).

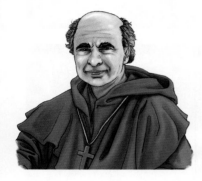

Friar Lawrence

Friar Lawrence's risky and complex plans finally end in complete disaster. The audience has to wonder why Friar Lawrence could 'dare no longer stay' with Juliet in the tomb as the watch approached. Is that a sign of cowardice? Does he value his personal reputation over his duty to the truth. He owns up to his part in the tragedy, but it is not clear that he did this voluntarily. Did he come forward or – more likely – was he found and arrested by the watch? The Prince seems to give him the benefit of doubt: 'We still [always] have known thee for a holy man,' but should we?

Death

At the beginning of the play, the Prologue described the love between Romeo and Juliet as 'death-mark'd'. In other words, it was doomed to end in death and that fate could not be avoided. Death is presented – ironically – as something alive and active and vindictive: it seems to take pleasure in destroying. This image of death is reinforced in the last act of the play. Romeo fears that death plans to keep Juliet as his/its eternal love object, 'his paramour' (Act 5 Scene 3). This is a shocking and revolting image. However, just as the play presents death as an active, powerful force, the final scene of the play presents love and beauty in the same way. Although Juliet is 'dead', Romeo imagines her beauty lighting up the vault, making a 'presence full of light'.

Romeo's love will go on forever too, thus defeating death. By killing himself, Romeo takes control over death and ensures that he will be forever with Juliet as her loving protector. This idea of continuing after death is echoed by Juliet as she prepares to kill herself by kissing Romeo's poisoned lips, causing her to 'die with a restorative' kiss: the 'kiss' will both kill her and restore her to Romeo.

Fate

Because we knew from the outset that Romeo and Juliet's love was 'death-mark'd', we are not surprised that they die at the end. However, Romeo both accepts his fate (he has been gloomy throughout) and defies it. When he hears that Juliet is dead, he pledges, 'I defy you, stars!' (Act 5 Scene 1). Rather than cheating his fate, he actually plans to defeat death by killing himself. His suicide next to Juliet

will – he insists – unite them forever. This desperate action will finally 'shake the yoke of inauspicious stars'. (Act 5 Scene 3). In other words, he has always been a slave of fate, but he will throw off that slavery by killing himself.

Justice

For the third time the Prince has to act as judge. He calls witnesses, hears the evidence and makes his judgement, confirming Friar Lawrence's assessment of the Prince as a kind and merciful man. However, the Prince, in his judgement, condemns himself for being too lenient in the past. He realises that if he had taken firmer action against the two warring families, then Romeo and Juliet would still be alive because they would not have had to hide their love. He decides that everyone has been punished by the results of their own actions: the punishment has come in the form of the sorrow of bereavement. On the other hand, his final pronouncement that 'Some shall be pardon'd, and some punished' might suggest that he has extra punishments in mind.

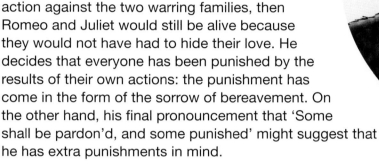

REVIEW IT!

1. Who brings news from Verona?
2. What reason does the apothecary have for being reluctant to sell the poison?
3. What is the name of the friar who should have delivered the letters to Romeo?
4. What does Friar Lawrence ask to be brought to his cell, and why?
5. Other than to see Juliet's face, what excuse does Romeo give Balthasar for breaking into her tomb?
6. What does Balthasar decide to do, and why?
7. Why does Romeo fight Paris?
8. How does Romeo kill himself?
9. What does Friar Lawrence find just outside the tomb?
10. How did Lady Montague die?
11. What does the Prince read?
12. How and why was the Prince punished?
13. Why does Romeo choose the apothecary he buys the poison from?
14. Why does Romeo call gold 'worse poison '(Scene 1)?
15. In your own words, explain how Romeo persuades Balthasar leave him alone at Juliet's tomb.
16. Why does Romeo ask Tybalt to forgive him?
17. Explain possible reasons why Friar Lawrence says 'I dare no longer stay' (Scene 3).
18. The Captain says, 'the true ground of all these piteous woes/We cannot without circumstance descry' (Scene 3). Explain what he means by this.
19. A watchman who has arrested Friar Lawrence reports that he 'trembles, sighs and weeps'. (Scene 3). Explain why you think Friar Lawrence is behaving in these ways.
20. What makes this last scene so moving for the audience? Explain your thoughts and refer to details.

Characters

Romeo

What we know about Romeo

- Romeo is the only son of Lord and Lady Montague.

- We don't know how old he is, but Lord Capulet calls him 'young Romeo'. His behaviour and how others treat him might suggest he is still a teenager.

- At the start of the play he is miserable because he is in love with a woman, Rosaline, who does not love him.

- He falls in love with Juliet at first sight and marries her secretly.

- He kills Tybalt and is banished.

- He kills Paris at Juliet's tomb.

- He kills himself because he thinks that Juliet is dead.

Romeo the lover

At the start of the play, Romeo is lovesick. He could be seen as overdramatic about his love for Rosaline. Some think that his love is more like a theatrical game than something genuine.

Here are two students writing about Romeo in Act 1:

Evidence

Notice how these students use evidence to support their views. They use two sorts of evidence: they refer to parts of the play, and they quote relevant words. Both students build quotations naturally into their own sentences.

Student answer A

Romeo feels as though he is as good as dead without Rosaline's love: 'I live dead', he tells Benvolio. His feelings must be real because he has not been going round telling everyone about how miserable he is. He has been keeping to himself - 'so secret and so close', so he isn't being an attention-seeker.

Student answer B

Romeo's moaning and sighing is over the top. Even when his best friend asks him what is wrong, he plays hard to get with mysterious explanations. For example, his days seem so long because of 'Not having that which having makes them short', and later when Benvolio asks Romeo who he loves he gives a long-winded answer ending with 'a woman'. He just seems to be playing games, and if his love really was genuine he would talk about Rosaline, not just about love in general.

Romeo the friend

Romeo shares the secret of his love for Rosaline with Benvolio. He also takes part in word sparring with Benvolio – and later with Mercutio. He is clearly used to these light-hearted contests with his friends. During one of these contests of wit, Mercutio falters and Romeo cries out, 'swits and spurs, or I'll cry a match' (Act 2 Scene 4). In other words, quickly think of a reply or I will have won. It is loyalty that makes Romeo avenge Mercutio's death.

Romeo the poet

Romeo is playful with words, but also he makes some serious and beautiful observations on love and life. The pictures he creates in the audience's mind are often clear and bright: for example,

> " But, soft, what light through yonder window breaks?
> It is the east, and Juliet is the sun! (Act 2 Scene 2) "

Romeo the grown-up?

Romeo is perceptive about fate, love and friendship. However, he is young and sometimes acts impulsively: he kills Tybalt in a fit of rage, and he nearly stabs himself in despair. '…thy wild acts denote/The unreasonable fury of a beast,' Friar Lawrence accuses him.

How do we feel about Romeo?

Surely, everyone will feel sorry for Romeo. He is passionately committed to Juliet and he does everything he can to gain happiness for them both. On the other hand he does have weaknesses, and tragedy might have been avoided if he had heeded the Friar's advice: 'Wisely and slow; they stumble that run fast.' (Act 2 Scene 3). Of course, how we feel depends on who 'we' are. Perhaps a modern audience would be more sympathetic to him than an audience of Shakespeare's time, when obeying parents was perhaps even more highly valued than today. On the other hand, love at a very young age might have been taken more seriously.

NAILIT!

In your AQA exam it is worth considering how attitudes of modern and Shakespearian audiences might differ, but do not jump to conclusions. Keep an open mind.

DOIT!

Look at this list of words that *might* be appropriate to Romeo:

unwise   unlucky   romantic   clever   reckless   brave   self-pitying   heroic   naive

- Think carefully about these nine words and put them into a rank order from the most to the least true.
- Find evidence to support your top three word choices.
- Might a modern and Elizabethan audience come up with different rank orders?

STRETCHIT!

Consider alternative interpretations for Romeo. For example, what could be Romeo's thoughts and mood just after Mercutio's death in Act 3 Scene 1?

Write some advice for an actor about how to deliver Romeo's lines at this point.

Juliet

What we know about Juliet

- She is nearly fourteen years old.
- She is the only surviving child of Lord and Lady Capulet.
- Her mother is still in her twenties, but her father is much older.
- Her personal servant has been her nurse since she was a baby.
- Her parents are determined to marry her off to Paris, a rich young relative of Verona's Prince.

Intelligent

Juliet is only thirteen years old and is carefully protected – almost imprisoned – by her Nurse and her parents, yet she is perceptive and often very wise in the way she handles other people. For example, she senses that her parents want her to marry Paris and she recognises how important this marriage is to them, so she is carefully evasive when her mother sounds her out about her feelings on the subject: 'I'll look to like,' she assures her mother, meaning that she wants to approve of her mother's choice. Juliet's reply cleverly implies respect for her parents, but actually makes no commitment. She is just as impressively evasive when she meets Paris at Friar Lawrence's cell in Act 4 Scene 1 – even though she feels 'past hope' of a solution to her problems at that point.

Beautiful

Romeo is instantly stunned by Juliet's beauty, which is 'too rich for use, for earth too dear' (Act 1 Scene 5), and he says he 'ne'er saw true beauty' before he saw Juliet. Her beauty seems to shine, and when Romeo sees Juliet at her window (at the beginning of Act 2 Scene 2) he says she is brighter than the sun, the moon and the stars.

Loving, loyal and trusting

Juliet's love for Romeo is instant and passionate. After her first meeting with Romeo she wishes aloud, 'Take all myself' (Act 2 Scene 2). She feels compelled to give herself to Romeo. She assures him that he can 'trust' her because she will 'prove…true' (Act 2 Scene 2). So although her love is instant it is also 'true' – loyal. Even when she hears that Romeo has killed her cousin, she still remains loyal to him, calling him 'my true knight' (Act 3 Scene 2). There is nothing fickle about Juliet's feelings, and perhaps this contrasts her with Romeo who shocks Friar Lawrence with his fickle love, swapping Rosaline for Juliet.

Here are some words which *might* be used about Juliet:

devious   independent   abused   romantic   strong   desperate   naive   honest

Choose the two words from the list above that you think are *most* true of Juliet. Explain your choices. Does your choice differ at different points in the play? Use your own words if you can think of more accurate ones.

Strong, determined, brave

Romeo has friends, but Juliet is abandoned by everyone except Friar Lawrence. A weaker thirteen-year-old would have given in and married Paris. First, Juliet fights back, refusing to marry against her own wishes, and then making up her mind to do without the advice of her traitorous Nurse. She is terrified of carrying out the Friar's plan, but she does not hesitate in accepting it as her only option for saving her marriage to Romeo. 'Tell not me of fear' (Act 4 Scene 1), she says to Friar Lawrence and asks him for the potion. He urges her to 'be strong and prosperous/In this resolve' and we have no doubt that she will be. Her terror is at its greatest when she is about to take the potion, but she controls herself, remembers the prize she will win through courage, and drinks the potion.

How do we feel about Juliet?

Juliet often thinks aloud directly to the audience – and at some length. She shares her secrets with us, expressing her hopes, her fears, her desires. She is strong and determined even when she has been the target of shocking verbal abuse from her father. On the other hand, the audience might disapprove of her deviousness and her disobedience to her parents.

NAILIT!

In your AQA exam, when you write about a character, make sure you make clear points relevant to the question and back up your points by referring to details in the play.

DOIT!

Look at what one student has written about Juliet.

a What are the strengths of this answer?

b Give the student some brief advice about how to improve their answer.

Writing about Juliet

Read part of what one student wrote about Juliet. Look especially at how the student uses evidence:

I don't know about Juliet. I know she's only 13 but a lot of what she does seems ridiculous and far-fetched to me. She thinks she is so much in love with Romeo that she's got to marry him or never marry anyone. We know this because she says 'My grave is like to be my wedding bed' if he is already married. I don't know who she thinks will marry her in her grave! It all seems so extreme. She says in the garden that Romeo overheard her 'true-love passion' but I just can't believe it. She's just obsessed like Romeo was with Rosaline. It's like they're both just playing at love. I suppose she's unlucky though because if he hadn't jumped over her wall then her silly passion might have worn off by morning.

Other important characters

Mercutio

Mercutio is a 'kinsman' of the Prince. He is neither a Capulet nor a Montague. However, his closest friends, Romeo and Benvolio, are prominent members of the Montague family. Mercutio is a complex character: as a joker, tormentor and word-dueller he is hard to take seriously. However, he is also proud, hot-headed and provocative. Shakespeare uses him to mock hypocrisy and posing.

Lord Capulet

Lord Capulet sometimes appears vague and confused. At the end of the feast he even forgets he has already had his dinner (Act 1 Scene 5)! Even so, he does not tolerate any challenge to his authority – whether that challenge comes from his nephew, Tybalt, or even his own daughter, Juliet. He quickly becomes violently angry. Shakespeare presents him as a model of patriarchal authority.

Lady Capulet

Lady Capulet, Juliet's mother, must still be in her twenties, given that she claims to have had Juliet when she was not much older than Juliet is 'now'. She is normally very hard on Juliet – for example, by abruptly telling her to marry Paris, and disowning her when she refuses. However, she is very distressed when she finds Juliet 'dead'.

The Nurse

The Nurse is a sort of lovable fool, twittering on, interrupting, repeating herself and referring indecently to Juliet's future sex life. She is very loyal, and her advice is sought by both Juliet and Lady Capulet. Juliet feels betrayed when the Nurse advises her to forget Romeo and marry Paris, but probably the Nurse is simply being realistic: she knows that the secret marriage to Romeo is a doomed romantic adventure. Through the Nurse, Shakespeare highlight's Verona's social hierarchy.

Friar Lawrence

Friar Lawrence lives a simple, holy life. He is widely respected and Romeo's affectionate guide and spiritual father. His agreement to Romeo's request to marry him secretly to Juliet is daring. He agrees in the hope that the marriage will unite the two warring families and improve Verona. Although his motives are praiseworthy, his plan is undone by the very conflict the plan was supposed to end: Romeo Montague kills Tybalt Capulet, resulting in Romeo's banishment and a fatal blow to the secret marriage. His desperate attempt to get the plan back on track falls victim to another stroke of bad luck and leads to the play's final tragedy. Friar Lawrence seems to be a mixture of integrity, selflessness and wisdom on the one hand, and unwise meddling and naive incompetence on the other. Shakespeare uses the Friar as the catalyst of the play's drama: everything hinges on his decisions.

Benvolio

Romeo's friend and cousin, Benvolio is cautious and always tries to prevent trouble, although he can be mischievous. His enthusiastic cry on leaving the feast, 'Away, be gone; the sport is at the best,' (Act 1 Scene 5) could suggest that he enjoys provoking his enemies. Shakespeare uses Benvolio to summarise important moments in the action and to highlight basic lessons, such as peace being better than conflict.

DEFINE IT!

catalyst – a person or force that triggers a crucial reaction. In a play the catalyst transforms circumstances from ordinary to dramatic

patriarchy – a society based on male supremacy

Tybalt

Tybalt is Lord Capulet's nephew. He is an angry young man who hates 'peace' and 'all Montagues'. His challenge to his uncle's authority results in his humiliation. Indirectly, his humiliation leads to the fatal duel with Romeo, and his death triggers the play's final tragedy. Shakespeare presents Tybalt as a model of arrogant male pride.

REVIEW IT!

1. Who says, 'you shall bear the burden soon at night', and who to?
2. How is this typical of that character?
3. Who says, 'I will make thee think thy swan a crow', and who to?
4. How is the speaker trying to be helpful?
5. Who says, 'Men's eyes were made to look, and let them gaze,' and who to?
6. What does this show about the speaker?
7. Who says, 'she doth teach the torches to burn bright' and about who?
8. How is this thought typical of the speaker?
9. Who says, 'O serpent heart, hid with a flowering face!' and about who?
10. Why does the speaker say this?
11. Who says, 'In man as well as herbs – grace and rude will'?
12. What does the speaker mean?
13. Who says, 'Death is my son-in-law, death is my heir'?
14. Why does the speaker say this?
15. Capulet calls the Nurse a 'mumbling fool' (Act 3 Scene 5). Write down at least three other things that the Nurse is called.
16. Why does Tybalt politely say 'peace be with you, sir' to Mercutio (Act 3 Scene 1)?
17. What could be considered Romeo's greatest faults?
18. Explain at least one criticism that Mercutio expresses about Romeo.
19. Choose *one* of these three characters: Lord Capulet, Lady Capulet, Tybalt. Explain how your chosen character could be seen sympathetically by the audience. You could consider how an actor might play the character to make them more sympathetic.
20. Explain which character – other than Romeo or Juliet – could be seen as the most important character in the play.

Love (and hate)

It is Romeo and Juliet's love that provides the dramatic backbone of the whole play. The word 'love' is used about 40 times just in Act 1! However, for Shakespeare, love is not only about romance and passion. It is a powerful force that takes a number of different forms.

Different forms of love

Here are some varied forms of love in *Romeo and Juliet*. Which characters, events and key quotations would you link them to?

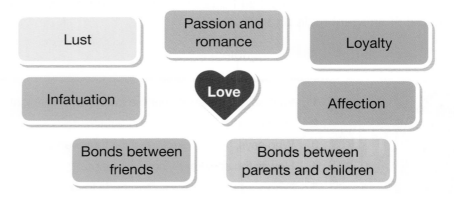

Lust

Passion and romance

Loyalty

Infatuation

Love

Affection

Bonds between friends

Bonds between parents and children

Is love a good thing?

Just as the play presents different forms of love, it also presents different *effects* of love. Most of us might think of romance as a magical and desirable state. *Romeo and Juliet* often shows romantic love as problematic: it is like a drug that makes people behave in foolish or reckless ways. Even when romantic love is not dangerous, it can be uncomfortable, painful even. At the beginning of the play, Romeo is suffering from lovesickness. Love rules Romeo and according to Benvolio it is 'tyrannous and rough' to him (Act 1 Scene 1). Romeo is tormented by love. He calls it 'a madness' (Act 1 Scene 1). Even when he is about to join Romeo and Juliet in marriage, Friar Lawrence fears the destructive power of love: 'These violent delights have violent ends' (Act 2 Scene 6).

Love is holy

Romeo and Juliet's love is passionate and instant, but they also treat it as a holy state: when they first meet they collaborate in extending a metaphor of prayer to justify touching hands and kissing (Act 1 Scene 5). The purity of their love is emphasised throughout. Even as late as Act 4 Scene 1 when Romeo has been banished, Juliet tells Friar Lawrence (a holy man) of her determination to keep her purity as 'an unstain'd wife' (Act 4 Scene 1).

The magic and beauty of love

Romeo's and Juliet's expressions of love for each other contain some beautiful poetry and **imagery**. Their love and Shakespeare's language are in harmony with each other. For example in Act 1 Scene 5, when Romeo falls in love with Juliet at first sight he says:

> " It seems she hangs upon the cheek of night
> As a rich jewel in an Ethiop's ear "

This is a striking and original **simile** that plays on the contrast between Juliet's bright and precious beauty and the night's dark background.

Romantic love and arranged marriage

When Romeo and Juliet fall in love, their love is so deep and entrancing that they are both quite willing to die rather than live without the other. Although their devotion to each other is admirable, it is not certain that Shakespeare – and his audiences – would be completely on the lovers' side: Romeo and Juliet's marriage is in defiance of tradition, the wisdom and desires of their elders, and good sense.

Juliet's parents want to arrange her marriage. Probably they have her best interests, and those of Verona, at heart. Experience probably tells them that the lightning bolt of passion is not a reliable guide for choosing a lifelong partner. Arranged marriages are still common today in some cultures so the central situation in *Romeo and Juliet* is still sharply relevant. The battle between parental preference and the romantic wishes of their children goes on.

Love and hate

As Friar Lawrence observes, love can be destructive. Even Romeo knows the destructive power of love in some of its forms. At the beginning of the play he notices the signs of a recent battle between the Capulets and Montagues and points out that this is evidence of the close connection between love and hate: 'Here's much to do with hate, but more with love,' he says (Act 1 Scene 1). The fierce love and loyalty within each family justifies and fuels their hatred of the other family. Romeo recognises the contradiction, but he also sadly notes how opposites can exist alongside each other and reinforce each other as 'brawling love' and 'loving hate' (Act 1 Scene 1).

DO IT!

Find at least two other moments in the play of 'loving hate' and/or 'brawling love'.

Explain *how* these are examples.

Fate

Right from the start of the play we know that Romeo and Juliet are doomed: the Prologue gives the game away when it informs us that the lovers are 'star-cross'd' and their love is 'death-mark'd'. How about those for spoilers? Clearly Shakespeare did not want the audience to be hoping throughout that the play would end happily; instead, the play shows the audience the unavoidable workings of fate. This suggests a very pessimistic view of life that may have been typical of Shakespeare's day, when early death was common and often sudden.

Just in case the audience forgets what they heard in the Prologue, Shakespeare reminds them every so often that disaster and tragedy is looming. These reminders are repeated foreshadowings of the play's final tragedy. For example, in Act 1 Scene 4 Romeo 'misgives/Some consequence yet hanging in the stars' that will lead to his 'untimely death'. At this point, Romeo has no particular reason for feeling pessimistic, but he is overcome with a sense of dread. In Act 3 Scene 5 Juliet suddenly gets a mental picture of Romeo 'dead in the bottom of a tomb'.

The audience should ask themselves these two questions:

Did people in the time of Shakespeare believe that they had no real control over the direction of their own lives? (See section on 'Power and authority' on page 69.)

Do people today feel differently?

Perhaps many people in Shakespeare's time believed that their destiny was in the hands of God. This is hinted at when Romeo is about to enter the Capulet feast and says, '…he that hath the steerage of my course/Direct my suit!' (Act 1 Scene 4). The 'he' is God, or perhaps fate, imagined as a conscious being.

DO IT!

Find other references in the play to fate and/or the influence of the stars. Here are two references to get you started:

> 'This day's black fate on moe days doth depend,
> This but begins the woes others must end.' (Romeo, Act 3 Scene 1)

> 'Unhappy fortune!' (Friar Lawrence, Act 5 Scene 2)

Although the play does end sadly and tragically, out of the tragedy comes good. Romeo and Juliet are a sort of sacrifice to something far more valuable than their love – the reconciliation of the Montagues and the Capulets, and a happier and more peaceful city. As Capulet realises, Romeo and Juliet are 'Poor sacrifices of our enmity!' (Act 5 Scene 3). A typical AQA exam-style question about fate might be:

DEFINE IT!

destiny – fate; something that is bound to happen to you

dictatorial – ruling by force

enmity – hatred

pessimistic – expecting things to turn out badly

AQA exam-style questions

- *[Starting with this speech,]* explore how Shakespeare presents fate in *Romeo and Juliet*.

- *[Starting with this moment in the play,]* explore how far Shakespeare presents Romeo and Juliet as victims of fate in *Romeo and Juliet*.

Power and authority

Shakespeare's Verona is not a democracy. Instead, a small number of men have a great deal of power. The Prince is the city ruler, and below him the big families have their own all-powerful male heads. The authority of these men comes from their power. Ordinary citizens must obey, and that means they – especially the women – have little control over their lives.

However, the powerful men are not always tyrants: they often exercise their power with sensitivity and kindness. Friar Lawrence tells Romeo he should be grateful for the 'dear mercy' the Prince shows him by banishing instead of executing him (Act 3 Scene 3). Lord Capulet, too, can be a tolerant man and a loving father. However, when their authority is challenged, both the Prince and Lord Capulet become dictatorial, angry and threatening.

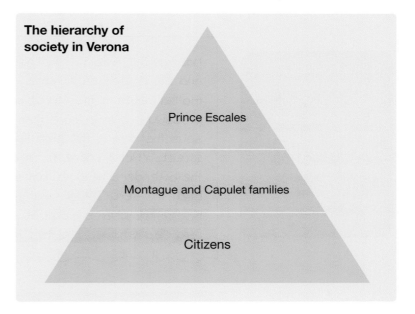

The hierarchy of society in Verona

- Prince Escales
- Montague and Capulet families
- Citizens

Other characters in the play have authority without power. This is true of the Friar and – to some extent – the Nurse. Romeo respects Friar Lawrence, and even the Prince forgives his part in the chaos at Juliet's tomb because, 'We still have known thee for a holy man.' (Act 5 Scene 3). A typical AQA exam-style question about power and authority might be:

AQA exam-style questions

- *[Starting with this extract,]* explore how Shakespeare presents power and authority in *Romeo and Juliet*.

- *[Starting with this conversation,]* explore how far Shakespeare presents Friar Lawrence as a figure of authority in *Romeo and Juliet*.

DO IT!

1 Choose a character – other than Friar Lawrence – who seems to have some influence and authority despite their lack of power.

2 Briefly explain how your chosen character uses their influence and authority.

Conflict and opposites

Conflict runs throughout the play. Until the 'glooming peace' at the end of the play (Act 5 Scene 3), Verona is in a state of constant conflict, but Shakespeare also suggests conflict is deep in individuals and within nature. This is what Friar Lawrence understands when he thinks about the dual properties of many of his herbs and he applies the same lessons to people: 'Two such opposed kings encamp them still/In man as well as herbs' (Act 2 Scene 3). So although conflict is most obvious in the Montague–Capulet feud, it takes many other forms, and Shakespeare presents conflict almost as the natural – and dangerous – state of things.

Montague versus Capulet

Read what one student wrote about the conflict between the Montagues and the Capulets:

> Notice how this student uses evidence (yellow). They make a clear point (blue) and then back this up with textual references (pink) which are mainly built into their own sentences.

Most of the time, the fighting that goes on and on between the Capulets and the Montagues is more in sport than for real. Both Romeo and his mother refer to the street battle in Act 1 as a 'fray', suggesting that probably it is little more than a boisterous mass scuffle. The Prince says that this is the third 'brawl' that has 'disturb'd the quiet of our streets' (Act 1 Scene 1). Although he threatens drastic punishments for the offenders, he does not suggest that any real harm has been done. Even 'the fiery Tybalt' who hates 'all Montagues' only 'cut the winds' with his sword. When a group of prominent young Montagues crash his feast, Lord Capulet tolerates their presence.

 STRETCHIT!

Looking at the student's answer, to what extent do you agree with this view of the Montague–Capulet feud?

Even if the Montague–Capulet feud is more pantomime than real, the play-fighting always threatens to get out of control. The feud is like a dry woodpile waiting for a stray spark to ignite it. The spark is provided by a chance combination of Mercutio's taunts, Tybalt's sense of humiliation and Romeo's quick temper. The deadly outcome of this battle prepares the ground for reconciliation between the two families.

Find some more evidence that supports this student's point of view, and/or find evidence that the Montague–Capulet feud is always real and dangerous.

Men and women

Much of the conflict in the play is fuelled by the fighters' sense of manliness. At the start of the play, when Sampson and Gregory are looking forward to a skirmish with the Capulets, Sampson boasts that he will 'thrust his [Montague's] maids to the wall'. He means that he will rape them as part of his humiliation of the Montagues. Women – according to Sampson – are 'the weaker vessels' and female weakness is also taken for granted by Tybalt when he accuses Benvolio of being 'drawn among these heartless hinds'. His pun on 'heartless/hartless' means that the Capulet women (female deer) are unprotected by men (male deer or 'harts').

Generally in *Romeo and Juliet* men are expected to behave in a traditionally 'manly' way. In part, this means controlling their emotions.

Friar Lawrence implies that Romeo is shaming his gender by behaving like a woman.

Women, on the other hand, are expected to obey their men: Lord Capulet and Paris demand that Juliet gives in to them as though her obedience is their right. Lady Capulet, too, although she is sometimes exasperated by her husband, has to obey him.

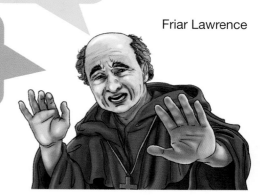

Thy tears are womanish

Unseemly woman in a seeming man

Friar Lawrence

Youth and age

Another of the play's ongoing conflicts is between old age and youth. Capulet tells his cousin, 'you and I are past our dancing days' (Act 1 Scene 5), but we can tell that he is trying to deny his advancing years by denying that his youth is very far in the past. He did this earlier, too, when he called for his 'long sword' to join the fight (Act 1 Scene 1). His wife mocks him by remarking that he needs a crutch rather than a sword. Despite her mockery, Lady Capulet also feels the advance of age. Although she must still be in her twenties, the sight of Juliet dead *again* 'warns [her] old age to a sepulchre' (Act 5 Scene 3).

The very young – Juliet and Romeo and others – keep their affairs completely hidden from their seniors, and their attitude towards these older people can be very harsh. As Juliet waits impatiently for the Nurse to return with news of the wedding arrangements, she attributes her slowness to her lack of 'warm youthful blood' (Act 2 Scene 5), and she complains:

> "...old folks, many feign as they were dead;
> Unwieldy, slow, heavy, and pale as lead."

Context

Context means one or all of the following:

- ideas and influences at the time the play was written
- ideas and expectations a modern audience or reader might bring to the play
- how an extract of the play fits into the whole play.

Using contextual information

Here are parts of two different students' exam answers. The references to context are shown underlined:

> ### Student answer A
> When Juliet 'dies' her father grieves 'all is death's' and Paris speaks to death calling him 'cruel'. This accusing attitude to death often comes across in the play. <u>It seems very dramatic and a bit ridiculous now, but perhaps people then were used to their loved ones dying suddenly and unfairly.</u>

> ### Student answer B
> <u>Shakespeare was in his thirties but he would die only about twenty years later. Lots of rich people had their own family vaults that they kept re-opening and putting their dead relatives in.</u>

Answer B will probably make you think, 'and your point is?' The contextual information given might be right, but it is not helpful. In fact, it is all context and no comment. By contrast, the contextual information in answer A *adds* to our understanding of the play by explaining why modern audiences and those in Shakespeare's time might react differently to an aspect of the play. A typical AQA exam-style question where context could be used might be:

AQA exam-style question:
[Starting with this moment in the play,] explore how far Shakespeare presents the Nurse as a loyal servant to the Capulets in *Romeo and Juliet*.

'Nurse as a loyal servant' is a clear focus of the question. How far she is loyal is partly a matter of *your thoughtful interpretation.* You *might* assess the Nurse's loyalty partly in the context of:

- the typical role and standing of a Nurse at the time
- what *you* think about social (in)equality.

NAILIT!

- For the purposes of your AQA exam, a context is only relevant if it sheds light on the play and the exam question.
- Answering your exam question carefully and thoughtfully is the best way and will help you consider the play's context.

NAILIT!

AQA points out that the best way to write usefully about context is:

- to make sure you answer the question
- to only include contextual information that supports a point you are making.

REVIEW IT!

1   Which one of the following is the best definition of 'theme'?

    a Something the play is about.

    b Music at the start of the play.

    c The order in which things happen in the play.

2   Give three other words that mean (or roughly mean) 'fate'.

3   Give three other words that mean (or roughly mean) 'power'.

4   Give three other words that mean (or roughly mean) 'conflict'.

5   Give three other words that mean (or roughly mean) 'love'.

6   Who is the ruler of Verona?

7   What advice does Mercutio give Romeo when Romeo complains that love is 'rough'?

8   What or who do Lady Capulet and Paris both call 'cruel'?

9   Why does Friar Lawrence tell Romeo he should be ashamed of crying?

10 Why do Juliet's parents favour Paris as a husband for Juliet?

11 Here are five themes: conflict, justice, friendship, power, fate. Which two of these themes are most relevant to the following quotation:

> "Thy fault our law calls death, but the kind Prince,
> Taking thy part, hath brush'd aside the law,
> And turn'd that black word death to banishment. (Friar Lawrence to Romeo, Act 3 Scene 3)"

12 Give three examples in the play of a powerful character showing tolerance and/or mercy.

13 Explain what Friar Lawrence means when he says:

> "Virtue itself turns vice, being misapplied,
> And vice sometimes by action dignified.' (Act 2 Scene 3)"

14 Give one example in the play of what Friar Lawrence means in the quotation above.

15 Read Romeo's speech that begins, 'O she doth teach the torches…', up to '…fellows shows.' (Act 1 Scene 5). How does this speech use the idea of opposites for effect?

For the next five questions, choose an extract of the play which is no more than 15 lines long that is relevant to the theme identified. Write a paragraph to explain the relevance of that extract.

16 The theme of love.

17 The theme of justice.

18 The theme of conflict.

19 The theme of fate.

20 The theme of death.

Language, structure and form

Language

NAILIT!

In your AQA exam, analyse the effect of a couple of relevant words or phrases in the extract. This is an easy way to show you can back up your ideas with detailed textual references.

When we talk about the language of a text, we mean how the writer *chooses* words to create effects. In other words, we are studying the writer's word *choices*. Shakespeare's language – although often brilliant – can be very challenging for a modern audience.

It's not as though Shakespeare was writing in a foreign language: he wrote in English, but – quite naturally – he was using a form of English that was more familiar in the late 1500s (the 16th century). Words and the rules for joining them up to make sense (known as grammar) change over time. If Shakespeare travelled forward to the 21st century, he would have as much difficulty understanding our version of English as we have understanding his.

However, Shakespeare was not just using the ordinary language of the 1590s; he was mostly writing in poetry, and he often made up his own words and images in order to express his ideas in fresh and engaging ways. These two aspects of his language can pose even greater challenges for the audience – and would have done even in his own time.

But don't be put off by Shakespeare's language:

- you can get by without understanding every word or phrase

- the effort to try to understand is worth it!

Look at these two very famous lines from *Romeo and Juliet.* Juliet is asking herself why she should care that Romeo is a Montague:

> What's in a name? That which we call a rose
> By any other name would smell as sweet. (Act 2 Scene 2)

DOIT!

- Choose three, four or five of the play's lines that you particularly like.

- Explain what those lines mean.

- Analyse why Shakespeare's language in those lines is effective.

Shakespeare's simple choice of language expresses a simple and important truth: changing the name of something (or someone) will not change its essential characteristics. The language is uncomplicated so as not to get in the way of a simple idea. On the other hand, Shakespeare's choices include some subtleties: the **alliteration** of the 's' in the second line make the idea more memorable, more quotable even. It is the *precision* of Shakespeare's language choices that make them so impressive.

Here is a student writing about the effects of Shakespeare's *precision* just three lines later:

> Juliet tells Romeo to 'doff' his name. I love this verb choice, 'doff', because you 'doff' a cap or hat, meaning a really simple, casual movement to remove it or even just change its position. Shakespeare has conveyed in this one word choice how small an obstacle Romeo's family name is - he could slip it off as easily as a cap.

Imagery

Some patterns of imagery are developed throughout the play. Such patterns include sex, death, plants and growth, and – very often – light and dark.

Look at some of Romeo's famous lines from Act 1 Scene 5:

> " O she doth teach the torches to burn bright!
> It seems she hangs upon the cheek of night
> Like a rich jewel in an Ethiop's ear… "

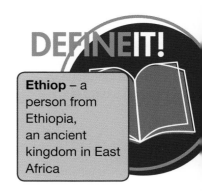

DEFINE IT!

Ethiop – a person from Ethiopia, an ancient kingdom in East Africa

These three lines lie within a vivid picture: a hall lit only by flaming torches, and the face of a beautiful girl shining from the gloom and reflecting the wavering flames of those torches. At the heart of that picture is a very unusual image: 'the cheek of night'. Those few words **personify** the night, giving it and the dancing scene even more life. But Shakespeare takes the Juliet/darkness contrast further by comparing Juliet's shining face with 'a rich jewel in an Ethiop's ear'. An Ethiop is, in the language of Shakespeare's time, a person from Ethiopia on the East coast of Africa, so in this image Juliet is a jewelled earring against the dark skin of an African person's ear. This is an original and striking image.

DO IT!

Re-read Romeo's three lines that were analysed above. Answer these questions:

1 Do I like this description?

2 Is it effective?

3 Do I *dis*like the description in any way? If so, why?

Be honest in your answers. Many of Shakespeare's language choices are original, but *risky*: they do not always come off, and not everyone likes every line – even if they like the play overall.

DO IT!

- Find three other points in the play that highlight the contradictions between appearance and reality.

- Make some brief notes on the effects of the language in each example.

The language of opposites

In Act 2 Scene 3, Friar Lawrence comments on the duality – opposites – that exists in all things. These opposites are deeply embedded in the play's language and imagery, sometimes in the form of striking oxymorons:

> " Misshapen chaos of well-seeming forms (Romeo, Act 1 Scene 1) "

> " Beautiful tyrant, fiend angelical (Juliet, Act 3 Scene 2) "

Images of contradiction and conflict such as these keep drawing our attention to the difference between how things look ('well-seeming') and how they really are.

NAILIT!

- In your AQA exam, it is *your informed response* to Shakespeare's language that really counts.

- In your exam answer, take the time to explain why a couple of examples of Shakespeare's language use are effective *for you*. Explain what you like about them.

Plain, direct language

Not all of Shakespeare's language is filled with original images. Shakespeare varied the style of his language according to need, and he was just as effective when writing lines that were direct and energetic.

Here, for example, is Juliet expressing her frustration with the Nurse's excuse that she is too out of breath to deliver the news Juliet has been waiting so long for:

> " The excuse that thou dost make in this delay
> Is longer than the tale thou dost excuse.
> Is thy news good or bad? Answer to that; (Act 2 Scene 5) "

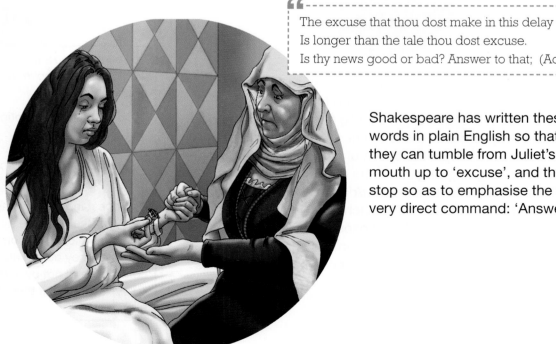

Shakespeare has written these words in plain English so that they can tumble from Juliet's mouth up to 'excuse', and then stop so as to emphasise the final very direct command: 'Answer'.

Structure

Romeo and Juliet is organised into five acts, each containing a number of scenes, and the story is fairly straightforward.

The three unities theory

Shakespeare would have been aware of the traditional theory that plays should stick to the 'three **unities**' of place, time and action. According to this theory, the action should not be over-complicated or sidetrack into subplots. The action should happen in one place and in one short time frame. The unities theory insisted that if plays did not stick to these rules, the audience would be unable to believe in the world of the play. Whether or not the three unities theory is a good one, Shakespeare often ignored it. In many of Shakespeare's plays the action is on a grand scale, moving from country to country, involving vast numbers of characters. By comparison, *Romeo and Juliet* is scaled right down. Its action happens in less than three days and takes place only in Verona and in nearby Mantua. There are no subplots: the action moves with hardly a pause from the opening fight to the tragic ending. To focus our attention, we are even told in the Prologue exactly what will happen. Clearly Shakespeare wanted us to learn from the play and he wanted to make quite sure that we noticed what it was we were supposed to learn.

Part of the **structure** of the play, therefore, is **didactic** – it is intended to teach us something. You may be familiar with these other didactic texts: *A Christmas Carol* by Charles Dickens and *An Inspector Calls* by JB Priestley.

1 If *Romeo and Juliet* is trying to teach us something, *what* are we supposed to learn from the play? Write down your ideas. Try to define the things we are meant to learn as precisely as possible.

2 Some texts are *very* **didactic**: they have a clear message for the reader or audience and are trying to change their behaviour. How didactic is *Romeo and Juliet*? Is it trying to teach us one very important lesson or a number of different things?

Tragedy

Romeo and Juliet is one of the most famous of Shakespeare's tragedies. A tragedy ends unhappily, but an educated Elizabethan audience would expect more than that: they would expect a tragedy to be structured in particular ways. Put simply, a conventional tragedy shows us a person of high status falling from triumph through suffering to disaster and destruction. The tragic hero often falls because of a combination of fate, the jealousy of others and personal weaknesses. Romeo roughly fits this model: he falls in ecstatic love, suffers terribly and eventually takes his own life. Fate (sometimes in the form of bad luck), his own reckless actions and the jealousy of Tybalt all contribute to his tragic end. Once an audience has identified Romeo as a potential tragic hero, they will not be surprised by each disastrous twist of the plot: it is all inevitable.

Audience expectations, controlled by the **playwright** and traditions, are a powerful aspect of a play's structure: if we spot that we are in a disaster scenario, we can simply focus our attention on *how* the disaster occurs.

Form

Shakespeare wrote in three different forms: prose, **blank verse** and rhyming verse.

Prose

Most of *Romeo and Juliet* is written in poetry or verse, but some of the play is in prose (prose means not poetry). Shakespeare generally uses prose for servants. Sometimes a conversation between high-status characters is also written in prose, giving the conversation a more down-to-earth feel than it would have if written in elegant poetry. For example, Act 2 Scene 4 is in prose. Here, Mercutio is bad-tempered. Probably Shakespeare decided prose better suited his mood.

Blank verse and iambic pentameter

Much of the beauty of *Romeo and Juliet* comes from the elegance of its poetry. Each line of poetry has exactly – or nearly – ten syllables and an even rhythm. This form often gives characters' words a thoughtfulness and authority that matches their sincerity. Not only are lines equal in length, but they are also based on the same pattern of beats, starting with an unstressed syllable and then alternating between stressed and unstressed. Below is one of Romeo's speeches marked up to show this patterning.

> "
> Amen, amen! but come what sorrow can,
> It cannot countervail the exchange of joy
> That one short minute gives me in her sight.
> "

The first and third lines are in perfect iambic pentameters. Line 2 stretches to 11 syllables, but Shakespearian actors may have joined 'the' and 'exchange' into 'th'exchange'.

DO IT!

Mark out the stresses (or 'beats') in the other lines in the speech above to reveal the iambic rhythm.

Do the same for two lines of **blank verse** in another part of the play.

Rhyme

Sometimes Shakespeare ends lines with a rhyme. This has a number of effects:

- it gives the line – and therefore an idea contained in it – special emphasis

- it can give a neat, firm conclusion to a scene or a speech

- it can make a line more memorable so that audiences recall it in later scenes where its idea can take on greater significance.

Rhyme, coupled with iambic rhythm, is particularly effective at emphasising ideas and moods. Here is an example:

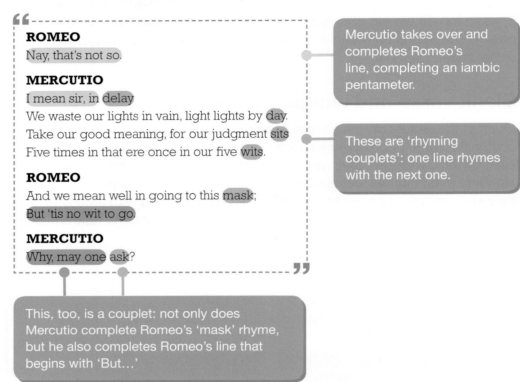

ROMEO

Nay, that's not so.

MERCUTIO

I mean sir, in delay
We waste our lights in vain, light lights by day.
Take our good meaning, for our judgment sits
Five times in that ere once in our five wits.

ROMEO

And we mean well in going to this mask;
But 'tis no wit to go.

MERCUTIO

Why, may one ask?

> Mercutio takes over and completes Romeo's line, completing an iambic pentameter.

> These are 'rhyming couplets': one line rhymes with the next one.

> This, too, is a couplet: not only does Mercutio complete Romeo's 'mask' rhyme, but he also completes Romeo's line that begins with 'But…'

Sometimes Shakespeare, using a technique called '**stichomythia**', makes characters complete each other's rhymes to emphasise the characters' unity. You will see this in Mercutio's completion of Romeo's rhyme above.

REVIEW IT!

1 What does 'thou' mean?

2 What does 'thy' mean?

3 What does 'hast' mean?

4 What does 'dost' mean?

5 When we talk about 'language' we are not talking about whether the play is written in English or another language, so what do we mean?

6 Name two good reasons for not being put off by Shakespeare's language.

7 What is a simile?

8 What is a metaphor?

9 What is personification?

10 What is prose?

11 What is 'blank verse'?

12 What is the term for a line of poetry with ten syllables that alternate between unstressed and stressed?

13 In this line and a half, spot the metaphor:

> O, I have bought the mansion of a love,
> But not possess'd it. (Juliet, Act 3 Scene 2)

14 Comment on the effect of the metaphor.

15 Why do you think the word 'possess'd' has an apostrophe instead of an 'e'?

16 How do the underlined words in the following quotation show Benvolio's urgency? 'For now, these hot days, is <u>the mad blood stirring</u>.' (Act 3 Scene 1).

17 Comment on the effect of Shakespeare's choice of 'bitterly' in these lines:

> Some consequence yet hanging in the stars
> Shall bitterly begin his fearful date. (Romeo, Act 1 Scene 4)

18 Explain what Juliet means when she complains:

> But old folks, many feign as they were dead,
> Unwieldy, slow, heavy, and pale as lead.(Act 2 Scene 5).

19 Find a place in the play where lines suddenly rhyme. Why do you think Shakespeare switched to rhyme? What do you think is the effect of the switch to rhyme?

20 Explain how the play's structure helps to keep the interest of the audience. Are there any places where the audience's attention might start to wander? If so, why?

Doing well in your AQA exam

Understanding the question

Make sure you understand the exam question so that you do not include in your answer irrelevant material. Even the extract should be explored *in relation to the question* rather than simply in terms of anything that grabs your attention.

Below is an AQA exam-style question. The question itself has been prepared by a student so that they fully understand it. Look at their notes.

NAILIT!

- In your AQA exam, the extract will come before the question.
- **Read the question before you read the extract** so that you read the extract with the question focus in mind.
- Read the question carefully and understand it. Make sure you stay relevant to the question.

The extract - I can agree and/or disagree (on one/the other hand)

How Shakespeare 'makes' Juliet

AQA exam-style question

- Starting with this conversation, explore how far Shakespeare presents Juliet as a strong female character in *Romeo and Juliet*.

Write about:

- how Shakespeare presents Juliet in this conversation
- how far Shakespeare presents Juliet as a strong female character in the play as a whole.

How does he MAKE us feel about her?

Other words for 'strong' – bold, daring, resourceful, determined, brave

Strong AND a woman – differences between modern response to her and in Sh's time?

This student has studied the question carefully and realised that:

- the focus is on Juliet as a strong *and* female character
- 'how far' means the student can agree and/or disagree or a bit of both
- 'strong female' can be considered from both a modern and an Elizabethan view
- our feelings about Juliet have been controlled by Shakespeare.

'Pinning the question down' in this way has allowed the student to make sure that they have really thought about what the question is asking. You should then use it to help you annotate the extract to allow you to choose useful evidence to support the answer.

In the examination room it is very easy to misread questions, answering the question that you want to see, rather than the question that is actually there. The method outlined here will support you as you begin to find some useful ideas to support your answer.

Nurse

Shame come to Romeo!

JULIET

Blister'd be thy tongue

For such a wish! He was not born to shame.

Upon his brow shame is asham'd to sit;

5   For 'tis a throne where honour may be crown'd

Sole monarch of the universal earth.

O, what a beast was I to chide at him!

Nurse

Will you speak well of him that kill'd your cousin?

JULIET

Shall I speak ill of him that is my husband?

10 Ah, poor my lord, what tongue shall smooth thy name,

When I, thy three-hours wife, have mangl'd it?

But wherefore, villain, didst thou kill my cousin?

That villain cousin would have kill'd my husband.

Back, foolish tears, back to your native spring,

15 Your tributary drops belong to woe,

Which you mistaking offer up to joy.

Nurse authority figure in J's life - brave defiance. Very strong language - almost abuse/violent.

Very grown-up sounding, formal - like the public words of someone in authority - iambic pentameter helps this.

Second time Juliet has turned Nurse's words back on her.

She reasons with herself, wins the argument!

Controls her emotions.

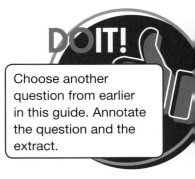

DO IT!

Choose another question from earlier in this guide. Annotate the question and the extract.

Planning your answer

Once you have fully understood the question, planning an answer will be quite straightforward. Your brief plan should set out:

- your key, *relevant* ideas
- the content of each of four or five paragraphs
- the order of the paragraphs.

Here is the same student's plan for their answer to the exam question on page 82:

Paragraph	Content		Timing plan
1	Intro - use the question prep to establish focus of answer		9.40
2	Explore extract - evidence of strength		9.43
3	Bravery - fear of tomb, standing up to father	Refer back to extract.	9.58
4	Determination - works hard for marriage and reunion with Romeo/assertive	Refer back to question focus/ sometimes. Question her 'strength'.	10.06
5	Weakness - position as woman (examples)/how *we* might feel about her.		10.14
6	Conclusion - brief return to question		10.22

Sticking to the plan

Note how this student has jotted down time points when they should move on to the next section of their answer. That way they make sure they do not get stuck on one point and fail to cover the question focus in enough breadth.

Planning to meet the mark scheme

The plan above suggests that the student has thought carefully about the task in the question, that they are familiar with the mark scheme for their AQA Shakespeare question and are planning to cover its requirements. (See the summary mark scheme on page 85.)

Assessment objective	What the plan promises
AO1 Read, understand and respond	Understanding of a number of ideas relevant to the main question focus – bravery, determination as well as weakness.
	Some personal interpretations to be included, suggested by intention to 'question'.
AO2 Language, form and structure	Exploring the extract will ensure close engagement with Shakespeare's language/ poetic form. Annotations already show this.
AO3 Contexts	Juliet's circumstances are harder because she is a woman.
	Consideration of how a modern audience might view her – 'how *we* might feel about her'.

NAILIT!

In your AQA exam, spend 10–15 minutes on understanding the question and planning your answer. There are no marks for using lots of words. Instead, you should aim to write enough *good, useful* words. Aim for four or five well-planned paragraphs (plus an introduction and conclusion if necessary). Practise planning as part of your revision programme.

DO IT!

Go back to the exam question that you chose for the Do it! on page 83. Develop a brief plan for it as above.

What your AQA examiner is looking for

Your answer will be marked according to a mark scheme based on four assessment objectives (AOs). The AOs focus on specific knowledge, understanding and skills. AO4 – which is about vocabulary, sentence structures, spelling and punctuation – is worth just four marks. Together, the other AOs are worth 30 marks, so it is important to understand what the examiner is looking out for.

Mark scheme

Your AQA examiner will mark your answers in 'bands'. These bands roughly equate as follows:

- band 6 approx. grades 8 and 9
- band 5 approx. grades 6 and 7
- band 4 approx. grades 5 and 6
- band 3 approx. grades 3 and 4
- band 2 approx. grades 1 and 2.

Most importantly, the improvement descriptors below will help you understand how to improve your answers and, therefore, gain more marks.

Assessment objective (AO)		Improvement descriptors				
		Band 2 Your answer…	Band 3 Your answer…	Band 4 Your answer…	Band 5 Your answer…	Band 6 Your answer…
AO1 12 marks	Read, understand and respond	is relevant and backs up ideas with references to the play.	sometimes explains the play in relation to the question.	clearly explains the play in relation to the question.	thoughtfully explains the play in relation to the question.	critically explores the play in relation to the question.
	Use evidence	makes some comments about these references	refers to details in the play to back up points	carefully chooses close references to the play to back up points.	thoughtfully builds appropriate references into points.	chooses precise details from the play to make points convincing.
AO2 12 marks	Language, form and structure	mentions some of Shakespeare's methods.	comments on some of Shakespeare's methods and their effects.	clearly explains Shakespeare's key methods and their effects.	thoughtfully explores Shakespeare's methods and their effects	analyses Shakespeare's methods and how these influence the reader and/or audience.
	Subject terminology	uses some subject terminology.	uses some relevant terminology.	helpfully uses varied, relevant terminology.	makes thoughtful use of relevant terminology	chooses subject terminology to make points precise and convincing.
AO3 6 marks	Contexts	makes some simple inferences about contexts.	infers Shakespeare's point of view and the significance of contexts.	shows a clear appreciation of Shakespeare's point of view and the significance of contexts.	explores Shakespeare's point of view and the significance of relevant contexts.	makes perceptive and revealing links between the play and relevant contexts.

AO1 Read, understand and respond/Use evidence

Make sure you read and answer the question carefully. The examiner will be looking for evidence that you have answered the question given. Do not make the mistake of going into the exam with an answer in mind. Knowing the play well will give you the confidence to show your understanding of the play and its ideas as you answer the question on the paper in front of you.

Using evidence means supporting your ideas with references to the play. They can be indirect references – brief mentions of an event or what a character says or does – or direct references – quotations. Choose and use evidence carefully so that it really does support a point you are making. Quotations should be as short as possible and the very best ones are often neatly built into your writing.

AO2 Language, form and structure/Subject terminology

Remember that *Romeo and Juliet* is not real life. It might be realistic in many ways but it is a play that Shakespeare has *created* to entertain and influence the audience. The language and other methods he uses have been chosen carefully for effect. Good answers will not just point out good words Shakespeare has used: they will explore the likely effects of those word choices on the audience.

Subject terminology is about choosing your words carefully, using the right words and avoiding vague expressions. It is also about using terminology *helpfully*. For example, here are two different uses of subject terminology, the first much more useful than the second:

> **Student answer A**
>
> 'Love's light wings' is light and airy, helped on by the 'l' alliteration, which might suggest a song-like 'la-la' sound, presenting Romeo as happy and almost floating in the air with love.

> **Student answer B**
>
> 'Love's light wings' is a good metaphor.

AO3 Contexts

Notice the emphasis on '*relevant* contexts' higher up the mark criteria. Here are some useful questions to hold in your head when you refer to context.

- How might the society Shakespeare lived in have influenced his ideas and attitudes?

- How might the society *you* live in have influenced how *you* respond to ideas and attitudes in the play?

- How might knowledge of the whole play enrich your understanding of the extract?

The best answers will include contextual information that is directly relevant to the *question*, not just the play. See page 72 for more information and guidance on how to make the most of contexts in your writing.

AO4 Vocabulary, sentence structures, spelling and punctuation

Make sure that you use a range of vocabulary and sentence structures for clarity, purpose and effect. Accurate spelling and punctuation is important too for this assessment objective.

Writing your answer

Getting started

Here are the openings of two students' answers to the question we have already looked at on page 82:

> Explore how far Shakespeare presents Juliet as a strong female character in *Romeo and Juliet*.

Student answer A

Although she is virtually imprisoned by her parents and she is nearly forced into an unwanted marriage, Juliet is surprisingly strong and resourceful. We see these strengths in every scene she appears in. But what is even more impressive is that she is a strong girl, and we know from the play that all females are at a great disadvantage in Verona. However, I am going to suggest that she is stronger than Romeo, despite his advantages of being male.

Student answer B

I am going to write about how far I agree that Juliet is a strong and female character. She is a girl really so her strength is even stronger really. You have to admire her for standing up to her father and mother and her Nurse and being brave enough to do the Friar's plan. Those are the sorts of things I'm going to write about in my answer.

NAILIT!

Introductions and conclusions are not essential. Write them only if they help you to answer the question. However, higher-grade answers signal a clear line of argument in their opening sentences.

DOIT!

Student A's is the better introduction. Explain why by comparing the introductions with the three bullet points above.

The extract

You do not need to write about the extract and *then* about the rest of the play. If you feel confident about it, then compare the extract with other parts of the play throughout your answer. However, a safer approach – just to make sure you do give the extract enough attention – is to begin with the extract and then make connections with other parts of the play in the following paragraphs. This is the approach suggested in the plan you have already looked at.

Here is part of that student's writing about the extract. Note the way they use the extract to closely examine relevant details of Shakespeare's language choices. An examiner has made some comments in the margin.

The Nurse must be a figure of authority to Juliet because the Nurse has been with her, looking after her since Juliet was born. Yet Juliet goes against her Nurse if she thinks she is in the wrong. 'Blister'd be thy tongue' she exclaims when the Nurse hopes that Romeo will be shamed by what he has done. Wishing in return that the Nurse will get blisters on her tongue is very harsh and very physical and leaves no doubt about Juliet's opinion: she is ready to stand up for what she believes in. This curse might sound a bit childish (and she's actually only 13!) but at other times in the speech she sounds formal, grown up and full of authority. The extended royalty metaphor she uses in the same speech ('throne'...'crowned'...'monarch') gives her words authority and shows her confidence in herself.

Direct evidence used well – built neatly into student's own words.

Effect of words is identified. Precise terminology

Useful terminology/ effect explored

Paragraph topics

The rest of your paragraphs should each deal with a subtopic of the main focus of the question. Here, the question focuses on Juliet as a strong female character. The student's plan suggests that the next three paragraph topics will be: bravery, then determination, then weaknesses. The 'weaknesses' paragraph will help the student to address the 'how far' aspect of the question: in other words the student can explore how Juliet is *not* strong at some points in the play, or in some ways.

Below you will see how – in their 'determination' paragraph – the same student makes references back to both the extract and the question so as to stay sharply relevant. The references are underlined to point them out.

> <u>Determination is a sign of strength</u> and having so much stacked against her <u>as a female</u>, Juliet has to show her determination over and over again if she is to have any chance of escaping from a forced marriage. <u>In the extract her determination is shown in the way</u> she talks to herself to control herself: 'Back, foolish tears'. She shows the same sort of self-control in the balcony scene when she suddenly stops flirting and bids Romeo goodnight. By doing this she gives Romeo a new sense of urgency so that he declares his love for her and she can then push forward on her determination to get him to marry her.

> This student uses direct evidence from the extract in the form of a quotation, but also uses indirect evidence when referring to another part of the text. Both forms of evidence are valid, but do quote from the extract at least – if only to show you can handle quotations.

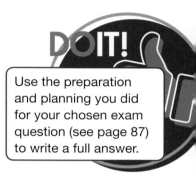

DO IT!

Use the preparation and planning you did for your chosen exam question (see page 87) to write a full answer.

Ending your answer

If you write a conclusion, make it useful: don't simply repeat what you have already said. The answer we have been looking at ends by summarising the student's personal response:

> On balance I think Juliet is a very strong woman. Her weaknesses are really beyond her control. Even a strong woman finds that she has to just do her best in the middle of lots of restrictions, and Juliet certainly has to put up with lots of restrictions.

In fact, this conclusion adds little to the student's answer and comes across as rather 'lame' when compared with the ambitious introduction shown in Student answer A on page 76. A better conclusion might have summarised what Shakespeare was trying to achieve through the way he presents Juliet.

STRETCH IT!

One of the ways you can ensure that you write a sustained and perceptive response to the play is by developing a range of evaluative vocabulary. Use words like: 'condemns', 'criticises', 'exposes', 'ridicules', 'subverts', 'questions'.

NAILIT!

In the month leading up to the exam, all your revision should be based on planning and writing answers to exam questions. You will find plenty of exam questions in this guide for practice.

Going for the top grades

Of course, you will always try to write the best answer possible but if you are aiming for the top grades then it is vital to be clear about what your examiner will be looking out for. The best answers will tend to:

• show a clear understanding of both the play *and* the exam question • show insight into the play and the question focus • explore meaning in the play in relation to the focus of the question • choose and use evidence precisely and wisely	**AO1**
• analyse Shakespeare's methods and their effect • use relevant, helpful subject terminology	**AO2**
• explore aspects of context that are relevant to the play and the question.	**AO3**

A great answer **will not** waste words or use evidence for its own sake.

A great answer **will** show that you are engaging directly and thoughtfully with the play and with what Shakespeare was trying to achieve, not just scribbling down everything you have been told about it.

The best answers will be RIPE with ideas and engagement:

R	Relevant	Stay strictly relevant to the question.
I	Insightful	Develop relevant insights into the play, its characters, themes and dramatic techniques.
P	Precise	Choose and use evidence precisely so that it strengthens your points.
E	Exploratory	Explore relevant aspects of the play, looking at it from more than one angle.

Below is a small part of a student's answer to the question about how far Juliet is a strong woman. An examiner has made some comments in the margin.

DOIT!

Find an essay or practice answer you have written about *Romeo and Juliet*. Use the advice and examples on this page to help you decide how your writing could be improved.

What strikes me about Juliet is how determined she is considering the sexist circumstances she is imprisoned by. Her father tells Paris he will accept Juliet's 'scope of choice' in marriage, but Juliet soon learns that her 'scope' is actually very narrow: she can choose to marry Paris or be disowned (a very apt word!) Juliet must know how narrow her 'scope of choice' really is, and knowing that might help explain why she is so 'quickly won' by Romeo: she sees him as an escape route from her parents' plans. Juliet might not even be aware of it, but perhaps she chooses Romeo as the lesser of two evils! Whatever the case, Juliet has to be strong and determined to win even a tiny bit of freedom in the sexist society of Verona.

Clear and nuanced point.

Precise choice of evidence.

Ironies of Juliet's position explored here.

Precise evidence neatly integrated into argument.

Original insight based on context.

Good return to question focus to maintain relevance.

REVIEW IT!

1 What should you do before you read the extract from the play?

2 Why should you do that before reading the extract?

3 How long should you spend on understanding the question and planning the answer?

4 What three things should be covered in your plan?

5 Why is it helpful to build timings into your plan?

6 How many paragraphs is a good number to plan for?

7 Why is it useful to know the mark scheme?

8 Should you write an introduction and a conclusion?

9 Do you have to write about the extract before writing about the rest of the play?

10 What should each paragraph of your answer be about?

11 Must you quote from the extract?

12 What is meant by 'evidence'?

13 What should be the focus of your revision in the final month?

14 It is vital that your answer is relevant. Relevant to what?

15 What four ideas should be kept in mind when trying to write a top grade answer?

16 Why is this a bad conclusion to an answer?

> So that is what I think - Juliet is a strong woman. I think I've made it clear why.

17 Why is this a better conclusion?

> So, in the end it probably depends on your view of Juliet. You could admire her strength for trying to escape the prison of her life, or you might be annoyed that she can only escape her father and Paris by giving herself to another man, Romeo. You could admire her strength or be annoyed by her weakness.

18 Here is an exam question. Annotate the question to help you understand it fully.

AQA exam-style question

[Starting with this conversation,] explore how Shakespeare presents a connection between love and death in *Romeo and Juliet*.

19 Write a plan for an answer to the question above.

20 Write one main paragraph that you have planned for.

AQA exam-style questions

On these pages you will find two practice questions for *Romeo and Juliet*. In the exam you will only get one question: you will not have a choice of questions.

PRACTICE QUESTION 1

Read the following extract from Act 4 Scene 5 of *Romeo and Juliet* and then answer the question that follows.

At this point in the play Friar Lawrence is speaking to Lord Capulet just after Juliet has apparently died.

> Peace, ho, for shame! Confusion's cure lives not
> In these confusions. Heaven and yourself
> Had part in this fair maid; now heaven hath all,
> And all the better is it for the maid.
> 5 Your part in her you could not keep from death,
> But heaven keeps his part in eternal life.
> The most you sought was her promotion;
> For 'twas your heaven she should be advanced:
> And weep ye now, seeing she is advanced
> 10 Above the clouds, as high as heaven itself?
> O, in this love, you love your child so ill,
> That you run mad, seeing that she is well.
> She's not well married that lives married long;
> But she's best married that dies married young.
> 15 Dry up your tears, and stick your rosemary
> On this fair corse, and, as the custom is,
> In all her best array bear her to church:
> For though fond nature bids us an lament,
> Yet nature's tears are reason's merriment.

Starting with this moment in the play, explore how far Shakespeare presents Friar Lawrence as a good man in *Romeo and Juliet*.

Write about:

- how Shakespeare presents Friar Lawrence at this moment in the play

- how Shakespeare presents Friar Lawrence in the play as a whole.

[30 marks]

AO4 [4 marks]

NAILIT!

- The question comes immediately after the extract.

- Read the question first.

- Make sure you read the extract with the question in mind.

PRACTICE QUESTION 2

Read the following extract from Act 2 Scene 2 of *Romeo and Juliet* and then answer the question that follows.

At this point in the play Romeo and Juliet are expressing their love for each other.

ROMEO
Lady, by yonder blessed moon I swear,
That tips with silver all these fruit-tree tops, –

JULIET
O, swear not by the moon, th'inconstant moon,
That monthly changes in her circled orb,
5 Lest that thy love prove likewise variable.

ROMEO
What shall I swear by?

JULIET
Do not swear at all.
Or, if thou wilt, swear by thy gracious self,
Which is the god of my idolatry,
10 And I'll believe thee.

ROMEO
If my heart's dear love,

JULIET
Well, do not swear. Although I joy in thee,
I have no joy of this contract to-night:
It is too rash, too unadvised, too sudden.
15 Too like the lightning, which doth cease to be
Ere one can say It lightens. Sweet, good night.
This bud of love, by summer's ripening breath,
May prove a beauteous flower when next we meet.

Starting with this conversation, explore how Shakespeare presents romance in *Romeo and Juliet*.

Write about:

• how Shakespeare presents romance in this conversation

• how Shakespeare presents romance in the play as a whole.

[30 marks]
AO4 [4 marks]

Glossary

alliteration Words starting with the same sound and placed near each other for **effect** (for example: *death-darting*; *bedaub'd in blood*).

blank verse Poetry that does not rhyme.

character A person in a play or story: a person created by the writer (for example: Romeo, Juliet or Benvolio).

chorus A device typically used in ancient Greek drama: voices (seen or unseen) comment on the play's action.

context The circumstances in which a play was written or is watched. These could include normal beliefs in the 16th century or the typical attitudes of a 21st-century audience.

didactic Designed to teach a particular lesson. Clearly Shakespeare uses *Romeo and Juliet* to teach the audience some things about morality and justice and the futility of conflict.

dramatic irony When the audience knows more than a **character** (for example: when Romeo at the beginning of Act 5 is feeling optimistic but the audience knows that the **plot** is heading for **tragedy**).

effect The impact that a writer's words have on a reader: the mood, feeling or reaction the words create in the reader/viewer.

euphemism A softened word or phrase used instead of a harsh, direct one (for example: *passed on* instead of *died*).

foreshadowing A method by which an author places clues about an event later in the text.

imperative verb A 'command' word; verbs used to give instructions (for example: *sit, think, understand*).

imagery The 'pictures' an author puts into the reader's mind. **Similes** and **metaphors** are common types of imagery. *Romeo and Juliet* is full of imagery linked to religion, death, night.

interpret Use clues to work out meanings or the feelings or motives of a **character**.

iambic pentameter A line of poetry that consists of five iambic feet (or 'iambs') so that the line follows an unstressed/stressed pattern (for example: 'If **love** be **rough** with **you**, be **rough** with **love**').

language The words and the style that a writer chooses in order to have an **effect** on a reader or viewer.

metaphor Comparing two things by referring to them as though they are the same thing (for example: Juliet calls Romeo 'a gorgeous palace'; 'Love is *a smoke…a fire…a sea*').

motif an idea or image repeated through a text.

noun phrase A group of words built round a noun. In the phrase the noun is the 'head word' (for example, in the noun phrase 'love's light wings', 'wings' is the head word and 'love's' and 'light' give specific information about the wings).

oxymoron Two normally contradictory words combined with each other (for example: *feather of lead*; *cold fire*).

personify When an abstract concept, such as death or fate, is described as a person (for example: 'Hath death lain with thy bride?' – Has death slept with your wife?)

(play)script The words written by the **playwright** for the actors to perform.

playwright The author of a play.

plot The story of the play: the sequence of the events and how they link together.

prologue Introductory words at the start of a play or book.

prose Writing that is not poetry.

pun A play on words that works by using two different meanings of the same word or two words that sound similar (for example: in Act 2 Scene 4 Benvolio says that Romeo will answer (accept) Tybalt's challenge to a duel, and Mercutio says that is not an example of bravery because anyone 'may *answer* a letter').

rhythm The beat in poetry or music.

simile Describing something by comparing it with something else (for example: The boy was *like an angry bear*; His running was *as loud as thunder*; It was *as yellow as custard*).

stichomythia Dialogue in which two **characters** speak alternate lines of **verse**. It was used as a stylistic device in ancient Greek drama.

structure How a text is organised and held together: all those things that shape a text and make it coherent. For example, Romeo and Juliet is arranged into five acts; it follows the sequence of a traditional tragedy; it has repeated patterns of imagery.

subject terminology The technical words that are used in a particular subject. All the words in this glossary are subject terminology for English Literature.

tragedy A form of drama in which a hero's life ends in disaster, normally through a combination of bad luck, fate and their own personal weaknesses.

unities The classical theory of drama that insists that plays must stick to three unities if the audience is going to be able to accept the drama: the play should have: one **plot**, be set in one place and not cover much time.

verse Poetry that has a regular form in terms of **rhythm, structure** and/or rhyme.

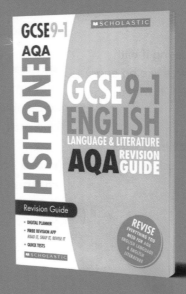